THE POWER
OF TRAUMA

THE POWER OF TRAUMA

From The Darkness Of Despair To A Life Filled With Light

Ute Lawrence

iUniverse, Inc.
New York Lincoln Shanghai

THE POWER OF TRAUMA
From The Darkness Of Despair To A Life Filled With Light

iUniverse books may be ordered through booksellers or by contacting:

iUniverse
2021 Pine Lake Road, Suite 100
Lincoln, NE 68512
www.iuniverse.com
1-800-Authors (1-800-288-4677)

Because of the dynamic nature of the Internet, any Web addresses or links contained in this book may have changed since publication and may no longer be valid.

ISBN: 978-0-595-46378-7 (pbk)
ISBN: 978-0-595-70155-1 (cloth)
ISBN: 978-0-595-90672-7 (ebk)

Printed in the United States of America

To my husband, Stan, my partner in trauma; my son, Marc, and my daughter, Natalie; my son-in-law, D. J., and all our good friends. You were there for us on those days when we most needed help.

To all those involved in the most horrendous vehicle pileup in Canadian history—to those who perished—may they be in a peaceful place. And to the survivors and helpers, whose lives will never be the same.

Thanks to Marceya McLamore (may she rest in peace) and the unknown gentleman who saved us.

May all of us find the path to happiness.

Contents

Foreword

Television has given us a window to the world, but what it shows us is often a world of violence and other upsetting events. We are able to follow the recent developments in wars around the world, hear the reports of brutal assaults, witness the carnage on our highways, and see the latest victims of violence on the streets. I used to be able to watch these reports from a position of emotional distance, but having worked in the field of traumatic stress for several years now, I find myself unable to stay in that protected and comfortable place. Now I am aware of the people who have been touched by these tragedies, and I know that when they see these events, they will experience their own triggers because of their traumatic experiences. For them, a simple activity like watching the six o'clock news becomes a potent reminder that sets off a cascade of disabling responses.

People with PTSD suffer immensely with wounds invisible to the rest of the world. Pema Chodron, a teacher of meditation, once said, "How did I get so lucky to have my heart awakened to others and their suffering?" Yes, I do feel lucky! With help and support, people with PTSD can recover and find their space in this world again. It is a journey of bravery and inspiration.

Ute Lawrence has shared one of those journeys in this book, and sharing a journey like this can be difficult. I believe that reading this book will present a wonderful opportunity for people to recover and experience the beauty that comes after a storm. I thank Ute for having the courage to share her experiences.

Nancy Wardrop, MSW, RSW
Traumatic Stress Service
London Health Sciences Center
London, Ontario, Canada

Preface

A traumatic event is a powerful thing. It takes you down into a dungeon of pain and despair, but it can also be an opportunity for unimaginable growth.

When I was diagnosed with PTSD (post-traumatic stress disorder), I started to research the disorder in great depth. Through books, the Internet, interviews with specialists, and therapy, I got a pretty extensive picture of the clinical aspects of the disorder. This did not, however, help me to heal the deep inner wound caused by having lost my belief system, my confidence, and the ability to function in my high-pressure magazine business. I experienced a gradual desire to isolate myself from family and friends, and my overall negative perception of the outside world meant that I did not feel safe anymore.

During my journey of discovery, I have learned a lot about who I am and my capabilities, but I also now realize that, like everyone, I do have human limitations. I needed help. I consider myself lucky to have been directed to therapies, treatments, and philosophies that helped me grow into a new, more compassionate person. It was not an easy ride, mainly because I was unprepared for the compounding chain of negative events that followed. I learned by living through the different phases of recovery, from the treatments from experts in the field, and, most of all, from my own extensive research. All of this culminated in a passionate desire to share this multilevel journey.

I realize that some people don't have the same opportunities that I did. Many don't have the understanding of loved ones, friends, and business associates to get them through those very tough times. That's probably one of the most important reasons why I have made it my mission to help others who have gone through life-altering periods of suffering—through education, awareness, and support.

I am not a psychologist, and I do not have an academic background in mental health. I am just a person who experienced an unthinkable traumatic event but came through the other side, just like many others can and will do. I am writing this book to share my personal experience and give hope to others that also have experienced the effects of trauma.

In this book, I share the long- and short-term effects of PTSD on myself, my family, and my career, to encourage others to find the inner blessings that trauma brings. I also discuss the therapies and information that have helped me, as well as information about the people I've met on the way.

It is my sincere hope that this book will help jump-start recovery for anyone who has experienced trauma, leading you to flourish throughout the rest of your life.

Introduction

Recovering from PTSD can be likened to how a tree heals after a storm. This analogy became very vivid to me as I looked back over where I had been. I felt that my roots were not just damaged by my storm—they were ripped right out of the ground. I later found out that my roots had also been wounded by previous traumas. I needed professional help to right myself, to get myself back up. So let me tell you how I see this, from the perspective of the tree.

After a damaging storm, a tree surgeon arrives to assess the damage. Work needs to be done to rescue the fallen, broken tree. Replanting it in the same environment, as is, would not be wise, since the next storm will bring it down again. The foundation needs to be worked on to prevent another upheaval. He clears the soil of anything that could impede growth. He digs deeper to create more space for growth. He adds fresh soil with the appropriate nutrients. He replants the tree, but not before the rotten or broken parts of the roots have been carefully pruned.

It will take time for the roots to reestablish themselves, and during that period, extreme care is needed. Once the root system begins to heal and starts to take and grow, there is a powerful chance for new life to not just survive, but to thrive, to expand past the limited space that was there before, unrestricted by energy-zapping obstacles.

I recently bought the book *I Can't Get Over It* by Aphrodite Matsakis, PhD, and I was very excited when I read that Carl Jung used the tree analogy as well. In her book, Matsakis writes, "Carl Jung, a student of Freud and a famous psychologist in his own right, used the metaphor of a growing tree to describe the client in therapy. The client, he said, is like a tree, naturally growing taller and fuller while its roots spread out wider and deeper into the ground.

"When the roots of a tree hit a large stone or other obstacle, do they try to shove away the stone or crack it? No. The roots just grow around the obstacle and then keep going. The stone may have interrupted or slowed the tree's growth for while, but no stone, no matter how large, can stop the tree from growing."

In Jung's view, stones in the way of tree roots symbolized obstacles to personal growth. These obstacles can include an internal emotional conflict (for instance, loving and hating the same person) or an external stressor (for example, a trauma). Jung theorized that certain emotional conflicts are not eliminated; they are simply outgrown. They remain as permanent parts of the psyche, just as the stones surrounded by tree roots become "part of" the tree. In the same way that roots can move far past the stones in their path into new territory, you can grow beyond your trauma.

Perhaps today, your trauma is frozen in time, far away from the rest of you. But once you have integrated the trauma into your life, you can use some of the powerful energy generated by the trauma to benefit you, to use in pursing goals of your own choosing. The trauma can become a vital part of your life—just as stones can support and strengthen the root structure of a tree.

Like a tree, you are resilient. With patience and support, your roots can be restored, and your branches will spread again. As the Chilean poet Pablo Neruda has said, "What did the tree learn from the earth to be able to talk with the sky?"

This is the brilliant and ultimate power of trauma.

CHAPTER ONE

Into the Fog

The day that changed my life

I used to greet each day with an almost naive anticipation of what wonderful things it might bring. I experienced a lot of joy and laughter in my life and, of course, periods of sadness and suffering. But overall, I always believed that I could handle everything that came my way, good or bad.

That belief was shattered one day. The most intense suffering I have ever experienced in my life started that third day of September 1999. My husband, Stan, and I were on our way from London, Ontario, Canada, to Detroit, Michigan, for a business meeting. The sun was coming up, and everything seemed fine. It was a beautiful, clear morning, and we were traveling on Highway 401, Canada's busiest multi-lane highway.

After stopping for gas, we encountered an unusual type of fog. As Stan described it, "it was like driving into a cotton ball." But there was just a small band of it, and then we were through, back to a crystal blue sky with the sun shining.

A little bit farther down the road, we encountered another band of fog; this one looked like a huge wall. As we entered it, Stan slammed on the brakes almost immediately, and we found ourselves sideways on the highway, just missing a huge truck in front of us.

Then all hell broke loose as an eighteen-wheeler went flying over the trunk of our car. Quickly, vans and cars slammed into us and into each other. We watched as people who had gotten out of their cars after their initial crash ran for their lives, being hit as more vehicles joined the pileup. The jolting from the cars behind was violent, and the crashing sounds were loud and seemed to go on forever. With each jolt, I felt it would be the one that would kill us.

It was horrifyingly violent. I had never experienced this kind of violence before in my whole life. Then came the eerie silence.

We started to look around, and we realized that we were trapped with no way out. I looked out my side window and saw an arm crushed against my window. It belonged to a fourteen-year-old girl who had been slammed against my small sports car by a van. She was pounding on the roof of my car with the fist of her other arm. "Get me out of here!" she yelled, but suddenly she screamed, "I'm on fire!"

Oh, no, I thought, *we are going to burn to death.*

The eighteen-wheeler that had driven over and crushed our trunk was wedged against Stan's side of the car. A van was on top of us. We never would have been found if the girl had not started screaming that she was on fire. I froze. I reached for my cell phone to call my daughter, Natalie, and to tell her and my son, Marc, that I did not think we were going to survive. I even had a quick feeling of regret about my new car. Stan and I were staring at each other. His eyes were huge with fear. I'm sure mine were the same.

At that moment, I looked up, and a truck driver was standing on our hood. He had heard the little girl, and he had brought a fire extinguisher to help her—and he found us. Stan yelled for him to break the windshield. *Oh, no,* I thought, *my new car.* He bashed it in to free us, just in time. The little girl was not so lucky. She perished along with seven other people, including her father and brother, who were trapped in their car just a few feet away from us.

We owe our lives to the little girl who died and to the unidentified truck driver. We will never be able to express our gratitude to them for saving our lives. And no one, helpers and victims alike, will ever forget the haunting dying pleas of the little girl. "I'm only fourteen," she had said.

This was how it all started for Stan and me. Here we were, a middle-aged couple, pulled out of our car with a few cuts. All around us was carnage. Yet by some miracle or fate, we had been spared.

So why did I not feel ecstatic to be alive? Shouldn't I have felt joy because we had been saved? That was not the case. That night, when we returned home, neither Stan nor I wanted to go to bed. I think we were both afraid that if we fell asleep, we would die. That night, and for many others to come, we drank copious quantities of wine to numb our fear, and we finally collapsed into bed.

The next morning, Stan went off to get some milk for our coffee. He could not leave our driveway. He sat in the car, crying.

When I read the newspapers the next day, they told the bigger story of the accident. The *National Post* article of September 4, 1999, cited the fog as one of the main causes:

"It was a strange fog, extremely dense from the east, which is strange; usually it comes from the west. The pile up involved 87 vehicles, including up to a dozen tractor-trailers, and the line of wreckage stretched for about two kilometers along Highway 401. At its center, 15 cars and 5 tractor-trailers collided before being consumed in flames. Many of the victims, still trapped in their twisted vehicles, some with roofs sheared off, made desperate, dying pleas as their autos caught fire."[2,3] This was the worst accident in Canadian history. It had killed eight people and injured forty-five.

In the days immediately after the accident, I started wondering about the events of that fateful morning. What if we had taken Stan's Jeep, which he had suggested that morning, instead of my Mercedes sports car? The eighteen-wheeler might not have catapulted over the trunk; it might have crushed the Jeep, because it sat higher. What if we had had the hard top down? After all, it was a beautiful, warm morning, and I loved having the top down. But as we approached the car in the driveway, I had said to Stan, "Let's have the top up this morning." What if I had not left my handbag and passport at the office? That was something I never did. We could not leave without my passport, since we were on our way to Detroit and had to cross the border into the United States. What if I had filled up the car the day before? When we got to the highway, we had realized that we did not have enough gas in the car and had to stop to get some. Would we have missed the fog if we had left earlier, without these delays? My mind raced through all of the possibilities as I tried to reconstruct the day.

Things kept coming back every night. The little girl's screams. The sounds of the crashing trucks and cars. The feeling of slow motion on impact. The fires. The smoke. The tires blowing from the intense heat. The desperate attempts by helpers to move my car to free the girl. One of the helpers trying to lift the car until the flames scorched his own face. My complete inability to think or to move. Our scrambling to get out of the car through the small windshield. And the fog. It had blinded us, captured and destroyed all of us in some way.

These images would haunt me over and over again for years to come.

I later learned that we had met three requisites of emotional trauma:[4]

1. It is unexpected.

2. It is something you cannot prepare for.

3. It is something that you can do nothing to prevent.

Like fog.

CHAPTER TWO

Aftermath
and Recovery

Before true healing can begin, roadblocks have to be seen and removed

It turned out that there were many roadblocks ahead for me as I embarked on my road to recovery. I didn't really know what was happening to me. I had the cultural misunderstanding that only veterans suffer from PTSD, so it couldn't apply to me. Trauma is life at its worst. I assumed that since an event was over, it was done with. Yes, it might have been over, but it was not done with. As much as I wanted to put that accident in the past, I couldn't.

The accident had happened on the Friday of Labor Day weekend, and the following Tuesday morning, I went back to my office. I was physically intact, and I assumed that I would take up the day-to-day responsibilities of running my magazine business. But very quickly, my life became a nightmare. There were deadlines for a couple of the magazines that were ready for publication. There were phone calls from the bank, which wanted the year-end financial statements that were due.

The insurance company wanted me to fill out forms to list the contents of my car that was burnt in the fire. Staff members were asking me questions about the publications and financial statements.

I was numb. I just sat at my desk, unable to think, let alone concentrate. I fiddled with my computer a lot, reading and deleting e-mail. It made me look and feel busy. But most of the time I just stared into thin air.

I blamed the distractions at the office for my lack of focus, and I started to get angry every time someone asked me a question about something to do with business. The insurance people were driving me crazy with requests for receipts for the contents of my car and questioning the prices of some of the items I had listed. "A Prada handbag worth eight hundred and fifty U.S. dollars?" What a battle that would become.

One day, I received a phone call from a bank employee about the financial statements, and I just lost every bit of composure. She told me that it had been two weeks since the accident, and she thought that it was time to "get on with it," because she needed the statements. "Get on with it?" I screamed. "I'd love to get on with it, you—!" I slammed down the receiver. I was shaking uncontrollably. I sat down and burst into tears.

Just a couple of weeks before this, I had been known as a highly focused, decisive businessperson, publishing a magazine in twenty-three different markets in Canada and the United States. That person was no longer there. I kept asking myself, *What is wrong with you?* I was—no, my life was out of control. I could feel a huge, charcoal-grey cloud around me. To make things worse, the cloud felt like the fog we had experienced on the day of the accident. I am sure that this triggered the constant feeling of impending doom over which I seemed to have no control. I was also troubled on my drive to and from work; I would jump and shake every time I heard the screech of brakes from other cars.

Determined to get back to how I used to be, I moved my office from its downtown location to my home. I felt that I would have fewer distractions and would be able to concentrate on my business and to "get on with it." I did not realize that this was the beginning of my process of isolating myself from the outside world, a world that was no longer safe and friendly, the way it used to be. Once home, I realized that the dreaded cloud was still around me. I was blaming the dogs, the unmade beds, the mess in the kitchen, etc., for my inability to concentrate. I would spend an enormous amount of time running from the bedroom to the kitchen to clean up. There I was, going back and forth, unable to complete the tasks. I was driving myself crazy.

Finally, in November, I decided to again move my office, this time to our cottage. Stan would drive to his office in London every morning and come back to the cottage at night. *Not many people up in cottage land in November. There should be no distractions now, no screeching of brakes to startle me,* I said to myself. During the day, it was just Dudley and Cleo (our two yellow labs) and me.

After several days, I had to admit to myself that I was just not the same person, which created a huge struggle within me. All I could think was that I wanted my old self back; I wanted to be normal. I was jockeying between numbness and hyperarousal. The intensity of these two states made my life a continual roller coaster. My thoughts started to wander off indiscriminately in all directions. One moment, I wanted to do something, and then I would change my mind in a flash. I was frantically out of control. It was exhausting. Friends and family came up to visit repeatedly. I could see in their eyes that they were deeply concerned, and they tried desperately to make me laugh. I would drink more wine during those visits. I suddenly felt uncomfortable with the way they tried to cheer me up.

One morning at the end of November, two months after the accident, I said to myself, *Enough, already!* I picked up the phone and called my family doctor, who immediately referred me to the trauma center at the local hospital.

What Is PTSD?

A fact sheet from the National Center for Posttraumatic Stress Disorder gives the following definition of PTSD:[5]

> Posttraumatic Stress Disorder (PTSD) is an anxiety disorder that can occur after you have been through a traumatic event. A traumatic event is something horrible and scary that you see or that happens to you. During this type of event, you think that your life or others' lives are in danger. You may feel afraid or feel that you have no control over what is happening. Anyone who has gone through a life-threatening event can develop PTSD. These events can include: Combat or military exposure. Child sexual or physical abuse. Terrorist attacks. Sexual or physical assault. Serious accidents, such as a car wreck. Natural disasters, such as a fire, tornado, hurricane, flood, or earthquake.
>
> After the event, you may feel scared, confused, and angry. If these feelings don't go away or they get worse, you may have PTSD. These symptoms may disrupt your life, making it hard to continue with your daily activities.
>
> Many people who go through a traumatic event don't get PTSD. It isn't clear why some people develop PTSD and others don't. How likely you are to get PTSD depends on many things, such as how intense the trauma was, if you lost a loved one or were hurt, how close you were to the event, how strong your reaction was, how much you felt in control of events, and how much help and support you got after the event.
>
> ### Symptoms
>
> PTSD symptoms usually start soon after the traumatic event, but they may not happen until months or years later. They also may come and go over many years. About half (40% to 60%) of people who develop PTSD get better at some time. But about 1 out of 3 people who develop PTSD always will have some symptoms.
>
> Symptoms of post-traumatic stress disorder (PTSD) can be terrifying. They may disrupt your life and make it hard to continue with your daily activities. It may be hard just to get through the day.

Even if you always have some symptoms, counselling can help you cope. Your symptoms don't have to interfere with your everyday activities, work, and relationships. Most people who go through a traumatic event have some symptoms at the beginning but don't develop PTSD.

There are four types of symptoms: re-living symptoms, avoidance symptoms, numbing symptoms, and arousal symptoms.

Reliving the event (also called flashbacks or re-experiencing symptoms):

Bad memories of the traumatic event can come back at any time. You may feel the same fear and horror you did when the event took place. You may feel like you're going through the event again as you flash back in response to a trigger, a sound or sight that causes you to relive the event.

Avoidance Symptoms

You may try to avoid situations or people that trigger memories of the traumatic event. You may even avoid talking or thinking about the event.

Numbing Symptoms

You may find it hard to express your feelings. This is another way to avoid memories.

Arousal Symptoms

You always may be alert and on the lookout for danger. This is known as increased emotional arousal. It can cause you to: Suddenly become angry or irritable, have a hard time sleeping, have trouble concentrating, fear for your safety and always feel on guard, or be very startled when someone surprises you

People with PTSD may also have other problems. These include: Drinking or drug problems. Feelings of hopelessness, shame, or despair. Employment problems. Relationship problems including divorce and violence. Physical symptoms.

My Journey Begins

Today, there are good treatments available for PTSD, and I've discussed some of them in Chapter Three. When you have PTSD, dealing with the past can be hard. Instead of telling others how you feel, you may keep your feelings bottled up. But talking with a therapist can help you get better.

I began my therapy with Dr. Ruth Lanius, who specialized in PTSD therapy; however, therapy was not an easy task. Before we could get to the traumatic memories of the accident, earlier traumas in my life popped up and needed to be processed. I learned that the body has a holding pattern. Peter Levine, in his book *Waking the Tiger*,[6] suggests that holding patterns in the body come from a response to fear or trauma in which an arousal pattern is evoked but not completed.

In May 2000, eight months after the accident, Stan and I found ourselves with a budding sense of self-awareness. Tentatively, we were beginning to focus enough to take our lives into our own hands. There comes a time in each person's recovery when this happens. A light bulb goes off. The clouds part slightly, and you see a sliver of sky. Be ready to seize this moment when it comes to you. It may direct you to a new way, a new life.

We decided to go to Canyon Ranch in Arizona for a conference on family business. We thought the retreat environment and the topic would be therapeutic for both our businesses and our mental health. Our instincts were right on both counts.

At Canyon Ranch, Stan and I were introduced to HeartMath and one of its stress intervention methods, called Freeze-Frame. This is discussed in more detail in Chapter Three.

I learned many lessons at the ranch. The predominant one is that when one decides to seek help, help will be there. It is almost as simple as that. The problem is that you don't think you need help initially. Of course, that is the best time to get help. So you tend to wait until the situation is extremely aggravated. My advice is to ask for help as soon as possible. Don't wait for the compound fractures to show up on the same pre-trauma path. But if you do delay, know too that help is there for you.

Identifying My Roadblocks

As I progressed through therapy, I discovered there were more road-blocks for me as I recovered. Each person will be different, but I had three big ones: what I call the Fight Club, my search for the spiritual side, and my cultural bias.

I had long been a member of the Fight Club. It's not an exclusive group. All of us belong to this club, courtesy of our physiology. In the early periods of mankind, the brain was wired for survival, for fight or flight. We could spring into action at the slightest threat, and thus we survived. I've always been a fighter, and that has turned out to be a blessing in some cases, because I persevere in making things happen. But fighting can be an obstruction in other situations. I'm starting to learn the difference. Fight mode can be dangerous if you are fighting your own emotions. This, in essence, is a form of self-destruction—a cascade of harmful bodily reactions follows. Heart palpitations, wild anger, panicky behavior, and violence may be part of this scenario. A terrible extension of this is that some of us become addicted to the high of fight mode and thrive on creating what Jon Kabat-Zinn calls "catastrophe living."[7]

The alternative is to join what I like to call the Flow Club. This is where you decide to go with the flow. You don't fight your emotions. You accept them as a part of the flow of your life, so you can deal with what is really important. What is most important to you? That is the big question. Is it to beat up on yourself or someone with whom you disagree? Or to listen to your own heart and share with a fellow human being? The answers to these questions are life drivers. What is your goal in your own internal life and in your relationships with others—war or peace? You have both possibilities within you; it just depends on which one you choose to activate.

This brings me to the next roadblock: my search for the spiritual side of PTSD. Believe me, it is there, and it is powerful, even for non-believers. I was not a churchgoer. I had lost faith in God as a nine-year-old child, when my father died. Back then, at my mother's prompting, I had prayed every night for weeks, pleading for my father to get well, but he died. I felt God had not listened to me, and I was afraid to pray from that day onward.

But one day, I made the strange decision to go to church. I thought that faith was supposed to be the bulwark of life. It was supposed to get you through the difficult times—and after all, I had been saved, so it seemed logical for me to return to the church.

I was craving some kind of spiritual pursuit, but my visit to the church did not do it for me. It actually aggravated my sense of despair. I now know from therapy that survivor guilt is a symptom of PTSD. I was suffering from survivor guilt, and my visit to the church did not give me any answers. I continually wondered why I had survived this crash and "God" had let a fourteen-year-old girl with her whole life ahead of her perish.

I knew that the foundations of my own belief system had crumbled into pieces. I wondered how in the world any of this made sense, and how I could reconstruct my life to include an abiding faith.

There is more about this in Chapter Three, but Dr. Dan Baker, a person I met during my quest for treatment, told me that people ask the wrong questions in the journey—they ask "why" questions that never can be answered. Getting stuck in these kinds of questions is a catch-22 and cripples your efforts to live a full life. Events happen and cannot be reversed. They are part of the context of being human. Living and dying are the two parts of the equation.

The real questions to ask revolve around learning from experiences. What did I learn from this? How can I apply myself to a life of greater fulfillment?

I realized that true restoration of faith relied on developing a spirit of compassion for myself and empathy for others, regardless of religious tradition (and sometimes in spite of it). And it takes time, careful sorting out to avoid the trap of fear or an overload of guilt.

I'm rebuilding the foundations of my own faith, stone by stone, well aware that the commandment to love is written on each stone.

The final roadblock was really a cultural misunderstanding: I couldn't have PTSD, because I was not a vet. Wrong. I had heard about post-traumatic stress disorder resulting from wartime casualties in Vietnam. Soldiers could not return to their normal lives because of the horrors they had experienced on the battlefield. They couldn't cope or function, and many turned to suicide, addiction, and self-isolation. This is a real problem with veterans in the wars of today. The association of post-traumatic stress with violence, like that in war, is still part of the popular understanding. But there is extreme emotional suffering from other events that can be just as debilitating. I am living proof of that.

PTSD can happen to anyone and can be triggered by all kinds of events. You don't have to be in a car accident, a war, a natural disaster, or a terrorist attack. Losing a job or a business, going through a divorce, failing at something, losing a loved one, seeing or hearing of a death, and experiencing cancer, childhood trauma or abuse, or any life-altering experience can cause post-traumatic stress.

When you have a traumatic experience, everything changes. You have no choice to return to the way things were, to old patterns, or to business as usual. The body holds on to the memories of the event and won't let go for a long time. For years, I continued to smell the smoke from the exploding tires and burning trucks. I could still hear the sounds of metal on metal and the cries for help. To this day, there are times when I am anxious when driving on a crowded interstate or highway, and I can feel claustrophobic panic at the slightest wisp of fog.

In Canada alone, it is estimated that there are some six hundred thousand people suffering from PTSD, and not all of them have been in an army, though perhaps they were on a battlefield of sorts. On average, 3.6 percent of U.S. adults aged eighteen to fifty-four (a whopping 5.2 million people) have PTSD during the course of a given year, according to the National Institute of Mental Health.[8] They all matter. We all matter. Trauma is trauma. It's a human condition. Most people experience it in some way at some point in their lives. Everyone will have roadblocks to getting on with life. Ultimately, thankfully, these experiences become the greatest teachers.

CHAPTER THREE

On to the University of Healing

Different treatments and programs that helped me come back and move forward

When I first started on the path to healing, I began the search for a new meaning and purpose in my life. My mistake, in hindsight, was that I wanted to get back to the way I used to be. I did not realize that the trauma had changed me forever. I should have accepted that this would be a difficult time in my life and that this was the one time in my life when I had to be on my own side. I needed to ask for support, learn to practice patience, and intentionally give myself time to heal. This is not an easy thing to do when your "fight or flight" switch is continually in the "on" position.

I have learned a lot since 1999. It has been a journey of discovery—of personal discovery and way beyond. I have been blessed to have people around me who helped me recover and become resilient again.

The statistics are clear. The National Institute of Mental Illness (NIMH) states on their Web site[9] that the rate of successful treatment for depression (70–80 percent) compares favorably to the rates for other chronic illnesses. The survey showed that many Americans do not understand that common mental illnesses can be treated most of the time. This includes PTSD. That's the good news. The bad news is that very few people know how to get the proper treatment. And sometimes, medical professionals themselves are uneducated about PTSD. They can downplay the suffering, especially if the patient can't readily identify the source of pain. They can prescribe drugs to mask the suffering and leave it at that. The doctors don't ask many questions, and trauma sufferers tell me that in many cases, the right questions are not asked.

In the final analysis, you've got to show up and stand up for yourself. If you have had trauma in your life and you are suffering from depression or any of the other symptoms mentioned in Chapter Two, it is important to mention this to a physician, even if it's painful or embarrassing. Please don't stop until you find someone. If one doctor won't help you, call another. Use your local phone book to find hotlines to get a referral. Each person has a different internal tipping point—the point where you won't tolerate your own pain any longer and need help.

In my case, two months after the accident, I was referred to Dr. Ruth Lanius, a psychiatrist and neuroscientist and one of the bright lights in PTSD research. She decided that I was a good candidate for EMDR and counseling. From there, I explored a number of other therapies and programs. There are also medications that can help. All of the therapeutic methods I will describe come at the issue from different angles, but they all lead to one conclusion: There is life after PTSD. Plenty of it. Good life. Abundant life.

I want to tell you briefly about EMDR, cognitive behavioral therapy, HeartMath, and positive psychology, so that you may see how these therapies may help. Please remember that I am not a medical professional, so my descriptions are based on my own experience and the extensive research I conducted over the years.

EMDR

EMDR stands for "eye movement desensitization and reprocessing" and is a method of psychotherapy that has been extensively researched and proven effective for the treatment of trauma. EMDR is a set of standardized protocols that incorporates elements from many different treatment approaches. To date, EMDR has helped an estimated two million people of all ages relieve many types of psychological stress.[10] The methodology was developed in 1989 by Francine Shapiro, PhD, founder of the EMDR Institute, and is being refined in practice every day. No one is 100 percent sure why this therapy works; all they know is that it does.

The underlying idea of EMDR is that a person can reverse the effects of trauma's extreme arousal (flashbacks) or total avoidance or numbing if he or she is exposed to two forms of stimulus—external and internal, physical and emotional—simultaneously.[11] The method calls for repetitious eye movements or tapping a part of your body as you talk with the therapist about your traumatic memories and feelings. The tapping helps you "always stay grounded in the present as you process the past," says Dr. Lanius.[12] It's easy to become overwhelmed by the images that come up during the treatment, but you are usually pulled back into the present moment, as she asks frequently, "What came up for you?"

As a neuroscientist, Dr. Lanius is investigating the difference between the neurocircuitry of PTSD sufferers and others through photomagnetic brain imaging. Sharing these images with patients is another way of physically locating emotional reactions, and that is another way to help keep PTSD patients in the present, where they are able to deal with their problems. For example, when I was shown the images of my brain, I could see how it reacted to certain emotions; when I was asked about the accident, my brain showed no activity at all, which was a sign that I am what they call a disassociator.

I found EMDR to be very effective. I didn't feel overwhelmed, but I was engaged. After what I thought was a much shorter time than I expected, my anxiety level dropped, and the lockbox of my memories was gently opened.

Before we could get to the trauma of the vehicle pileup, images of earlier traumas came up during the treatments. My father died when I was nine. My mother didn't want me to go to the funeral. She wanted to protect me from bad experiences, and she was harsh with me when I did something wrong. In my later life, I had completely reconciled with my mother. So when these earlier conflicts arose in treatment, I experienced very strong emotions, mainly anger and sadness. Once I was in touch with my repressed anger and sadness, I finally processed the experiences and was relieved of their residue.

After a series of treatments, I started to reconnect with my own resources, and I could feel a reframing of my present life. I felt a new me being born.

Cognitive Behavioral Therapy

In his book *Healthy Aging*, Andrew Weil, MD, explains that cognitive behavioral therapy (CBT) "has become popular only in recent years. It traces its remote origins to the teachings of the Buddha and a Greek philosopher, Epictetus, who developed a science of happiness. He taught people to live in accordance with nature, to unlearn the habit of judging everything that happens as good or bad, and to learn to distinguish what is in your power to change and what is not. 'Make the best of what is in your power, take the rest as it comes,' is one quote attributed to him."[13]

CBT appears to be the most effective type of counseling for PTSD.[14]

Psychologist Dr. William Newby[15] practices CBT, and he says, "Anxiety disorders are very treatable, but best treated when they are fresh." That's also a message to seek help early on. Dr. Newby's approach is to help patients integrate the traumatic experience into themselves through exposure, going over the trauma to strip away the horror. He calls PTSD a bubble of undiagnosed experience, something that exists without a context. He says that this makes it potentially life-threatening, because you can't absorb it into your sense of yourself and your world. "My job," he says, "is to help patients massage this experience into their reality."

Dr. Newby explains that CBT is a form of psychotherapy that emphasizes the key role of thinking in how you feel and what you do. It is based on the scientific fact that thoughts cause feelings and behaviors; feelings and behaviors are not caused by external things, like people, situations, and events. In other words, the priority for CBT is a healthy way of processing events, because it is control central for what you feel and how you act. The great benefit is that you can change the way you think to feel and act better, even if the situation stays the same.

Most people who go into therapy don't like the way they feel. You are hurting and can't seem to understand the source or alleviate the pain. CBT is a structured, fairly short-term form of rational therapy to get at both cause and effect. I responded very well, because it made sense.

Throughout the therapy, Dr. Newby asked me questions. These questions made me rethink what had happened and what I was doing about it. I could start connecting the dots of my experience. But most importantly, I learned to rethink how I was looking at myself, the expectations I had for myself. I learned to stop continually judging myself and, I hate to say, others. Then I would practice these techniques at home. I found that I could stay calmer in crises, because I could sort out the facts more clearly. I could get things straight and focus more on the reality of the present. All of this bolstered my confidence that I could retrain my brain to break some of the thought patterns that did not serve me well. I was gaining incredible insight into my own way of dealing with myself and others.

But the most important thing I discovered from this therapy is that I am no different from anybody else. As Dr. Newby said to me during a session, "Ute, you do belong, because guess what? You are as screwed up as the rest of us." This statement really hit home. It had an incredibly liberating effect on me and allowed me, bit by bit, to drop my desire to be perfect all the time.

During my first visit, Dr. Newby gave me Jon Kabat-Zinn's book *Wherever You Go, There You Are,* which describes many different meditations and how to learn to meditate. He also gave me a meditation CD. He encouraged me to start meditating—very difficult for someone with PTSD. But through practice, minute by minute, I was able to increase the stillness. When I did that, I found it easier to find the answers that I was seeking.

HeartMath

The Institute of HeartMath was founded in 1991 by Doc Childre to research the effect of mental and emotional stress on the heart, brain, and nervous system.[16] The Institute of HeartMath has focused its research on the critical link between emotions, heart function, and cognitive performance. Its mission is to help people establish heart-based living by teaching them to connect with the intelligence of their hearts.[17]

Just think of the ever-pumping heart—an extraordinary energy and deep force inside every one of us. It can work without interruption for seventy to eighty years without care or cleaning, without repair or replacement. Day and night, it beats one hundred thousand times a day—approximately forty million times a year—and in seventy years, it will have completed nearly three billion cardiac pulsations. It pumps two gallons of blood a minute—one hundred gallons an hour—through a vascular system that's sixty thousand miles in length, which is two and a half times the circumference of the Earth!

Scientific research[18] shows that the heart has its own independent nervous system with some forty thousand neurons, referred to as the "brain in the heart." Research also shows that the heart's most ardent enemy is stress. Stress poisons you. Every single stressful event floods us with stress hormones, which are as harmful to our bodies as rivers of acid. The more stress, the more difficult it is for your cardiovascular system and your brain to function well. Post-traumatic stress is extreme and dangerous.

And did you know that there's another heart, your inner heart? And that holds the biggest surprise of all. You'll find that your most reliant guide, your most loyal ally, and the truest wisdom reside not in your mind alone, but right in the center of your being—in your heart.

Researcher, author, and consultant Doc Childre has devoted more than thirty years to understanding stress and developing ways to transform its effects. During those decades, he discovered something remarkably simple. He found that positive thinking creates stress relief, but only temporarily. However, Childre and his research team found that by also engaging the heart and creating positive feelings, stress relief is more sustainable and can also actually reverse the physical damage of stress.

When you consciously shift to feeling appreciation, compassion, or other positive, loving emotions, your heart rhythm immediately shifts. This shift in rhythm creates a favorable cascade of neural, hormonal, and biochemical events that benefit the entire body. Blood pressure normalizes. Stress hormones plummet. The immune system pumps up. Anti-aging hormones increase. You gain clarity, calmness, and control, and the effects are both immediate and long lasting. Based on these validated results, Doc Childre developed HeartMath, which is a system of programs, techniques, and technologies designed to prevent, manage, and reverse the effects of stress.

HeartMath's research director, Dr. Rollin McCraty, says, "Emotions run the show." He points out that current neuroscientific research shows that emotional experience is a body-wide process, with the heart sending more information to the brain than the brain sends to the heart. How does this affect HeartMath's therapeutic model for PTSD, where the imprint of trauma is so strong that it keeps coming back although the traumatic event itself is over?

HeartMath's approach is to start with healing the emotional heart first. You can take the charge out of the flashbacks by managing your own physiology through breathing and changing your thoughts to positive, loving emotions. One of the myths of recovery is that you don't have control over your emotions. PTSD is an emotional response, and you can start taking steps toward empowerment by changing how you respond.

HeartMath Institute psychologist Dr. Deborah Rozman says, "Many clinical social workers are using HeartMath's stress solutions with soldiers suffering from PTSD. The results have been excellent and are giving soldiers a chance to start fresh as they reintegrate into civilian life."

You don't forget the event, but eventually, you learn to recognize what triggers your flashbacks or anxious symptoms, and when triggers arise, you can start using HeartMath tools to change your reaction. I found the Freeze-Frame tool to be very effective. "The term 'freeze frame' is movie lingo for stopping a film at a single frame to take a closer look. We have to stop the projector and freeze the frame."[19]

Here are the five steps of the Freeze-Frame technique:

1. Recognize the stressful feeling, and Freeze-Frame it. *Take a time-out!*

2. Make a sincere effort to shift your focus away from the racing mind or disturbed emotions to the area around your heart. You can pretend that you're breathing through your heart to help focus your energy in this area. Keep your focus there for then seconds or more.

3. Recall a positive, fun feeling or time you've had in life and attempt to re-experience it.

4. Now, using your intuition, common sense and sincerity, ask your heart what would be a more efficient response to the situation, one that will minimize future stress.

5. Listen to what your heart says in answer to your question. It's an effective way to put your reactive mind and emotions in check—and an "in-house" source of common-sense solutions![20]

The fast-beating heart begins to slow down and the brain gets a different message, which it then sends to the rest of the body.

One of the great lessons I learned with this program is that if you have PTSD, you need to retrain yourself, reset your neuropatterns as you recover. With these tools, the heart sends a different message to the brain, and the brain labels it good. The result is a state of clarity replacing chaos, a feeling of coherence overriding confusion. "People can learn not to let the floodgates of emotional trauma control them," says Dr. Rozman.

I think HeartMath works. HeartMath and its stress intervention tools (like Freeze-Frame) have had a major effect on my daily reduction of stress. In 2001, I took a telecourse on how to use the tools and became so fascinated with the subject, the tools, and the knowledge that I decided to take a training course at the Institute of HeartMath in Boulder Creek, California, to become a licensed one-on-one Heart-Math provider so I could teach the course myself.

Like all therapies, this is not a magic bullet. It takes practice and intent, but it gives you a step-by-step tool. You can do this.

Positive Psychology

Dan Baker, PhD,[21] is the founder and former director of the Life Enhancement Program at Canyon Ranch Health Resort in Arizona. As I mentioned before, Stan and I went there as part of our healing journey. He is a proponent of positive psychology,[22] which is "a new branch of psychology which focuses on the empirical study of such things as positive emotions and strengths-based character. Dr. Martin Seligman is the founder of positive psychology and his research has demonstrated that it is possible to be happier—to feel more satisfied, to be more engaged with life, find more meaning, have higher hopes, and probably even laugh and smile more, regardless of one's circumstances. Positive psychology interventions can also lastingly decrease depression symptoms." This therapy has emerged in the palette of therapies in the last five or six years, and Dr. Baker uses this positive approach to leading a meaningful life. Baker has written three books on the subject of happiness for people and for companies. He explained to me, "You will never see a truly happy and simultaneously hostile person, because those two states are essentially neurologically incompatible." In other words, happiness is just as attainable as its opposite. It is your choice, ultimately.

Because questions have implicit direction and take you somewhere, Baker asserts that you should not ask "Why me?" because it takes one into the darkness, to a passive state dangerously close to being a victim. There is no satisfactory answer to this question. Life is riddled with tragedy, and sometimes it is ours. However, there are major questions that Baker says can and should be asked at this time:

"What is my lesson?"
"What am I to learn from this?
"How do I become wiser? More resilient?"
"How can I appreciate what I have had prior to this that allows me to cope with what I have lost?"

Baker synonymously uses the adjective "constructive" with the word "positive" to describe a happy person. He or she doesn't acquiesce to the trauma by prolonging passivity, continuing to blame others, or choosing to stay in the misery. We have all been to these places, and they are black holes. As Baker pointed out to me, "Passivity creates inertia. Blaming passes the buck. Self-pity can't coexist with self-esteem." How true!

In dealing with PTSD, this new avenue of therapy does not discount the residual memory of the event. It understands that it will stay lodged in the deeper, lower parts of the brain. Humans are still wired for hard times. The "fight, flight, or freeze" reaction is always with us. But with the right skills, trauma's harmful emotional and physical effects can, after the fact, be overruled by a positive, conscious reordering of your psychology. And time has given humans the wonderful adaptive features of the frontal lobe, which is part of the cerebral cortex, the most highly developed area of the brain; it continues to develop new neural circuits or networks throughout a person's life.[23] Dr. Baker calls this "the highest achievement of human brain evolution." This is where your positive emotions can be evoked, especially when false alarms go off.

Some of us have a larger reserve than others, but all of us have some experience with joy. A loving touch, a word of thanks, a helping hand—you can underestimate the power of these gestures and their promise of a good life.

This downplaying of the positive is part of the heritage of allopathic medicine, which means "against pathology." In other words, if you are not sick, you must be well. "It never entertains the pro-health question of seeking a highly vital and robust life," says Baker. "This is where positive psychology comes into play. It really asks the question 'how can people thrive?'"

Another assumption of this new psychology is that we are all in this together. You don't live in a vacuum. The more you learn how your life affects those of others, the better off everyone will be. Psychologist Paul Pearsall[24] puts it this way in his book *The Beethoven Factor*: "Thriving is a total mind-body-others life system." Baker talks of the three elements that lead to a diversified psychosocial portfolio for happiness: a sense of purpose, health as the optimal condition of being, and relationships.

Life is fragile. I knew that before my accident, but the trauma brought that home to me in a way I could not have understood before. I have learned that I am responsible for managing myself, my behavior, my thoughts—and my emotions. Do you want to look at the glass as half empty or half full? Are you waiting for the other shoe to fall, or do you appreciate that wherever you go, there you are? Those are the main questions to ask when you are stuck. The answers can determine the course of the rest of your life.

CHAPTER FOUR

Three People I Met on My Way

Trauma survivors share their stories to show the common bond

PTSD can manifest itself in different ways and because of different causes. I'd like to share the stories of James,[25] Dave,[26] and Suzanne,[27] to show those differences and encourage you on your journey. I met them at different times while I was already well on my way to recovery and had the privilege to share with them some of my own experiences and the treatments that helped me. James and Dave had suffered from traumatic events and unknowingly suffered from PTSD, and the symptoms were left untreated. Both of them were at the point of having breakdowns when I came into their lives, and I was able to direct them to the treatments that had helped me. I had met Suzanne in 2002, but the cruel murder of her brother in 2006 changed her life. All three are wonderful, dynamic, and courageous people, and I am grateful to have played a small part in helping them find the help they needed and equally grateful that they have become a part of my life.

James

James Vail is a systems analyst and a single father of four living in London, Ontario. He describes himself as "a casualty of the war on terror." James was working in New York on September 11, 2001; he told me that this day defined his life forever.

Just after 8:46 am, he stepped off the subway at the World Trade Center stop on his way to work. He had taken the seven-minute ride to work from the New Jersey side of the Hudson River. He heard some unusual snapping sounds from somewhere in the underground hub, and a faint smell of electricity was in the air. He figured that a construction worker probably had made a mistake. He stopped to buy a hot chocolate and a newspaper and headed toward the escalators.

When he reached ground level, a policeman yelled, "Get out of here!" No one paid much attention, but suddenly there was a big bang, and smoke filled the foyer. People started to run. James moved toward the Liberty Street exit, where he saw two elderly women struggling in front of him. He approached them and took them by the arms, and the linked threesome moved toward the door.

Outside, it appeared to be snowing, but what was falling was burning paper, and the street was covered in debris—glass, chunks of concrete, and more paper. He found a safe doorway where the women could be protected and then proceeded to his workplace a few blocks away at the One World Financial Center across the street from the Twin Towers.

He heard that a plane had flown into a building. It was now 9:00 am. "There was crap falling all over me," he said. Looking up at the building that was burning like a candle, he thought, *Why aren't the sprinklers working?* Then he heard a strange roar. A huge passenger plane came from the south and plowed into the second tower. People were screaming. Some fell to the ground. An officer told everyone to get out. James ran to his own building, and his colleagues were running out of it, telling him to turn around.

One image is seared into his memory. A woman appeared, hundreds of meters up, in the hole created by the plane. She and her partner were holding hands, and slowly they made their way to the ledge of the window. They held hands all the way down. "It sounded like a sack of potatoes," he said. "Here were two human beings who wanted to be together. They expressed a faith in each other. Whether they were married or not … does it matter? If they were friends, they were the best of friends."

James was overwhelmed. He finally got a ferry out of the city at about 10:00 am. Halfway across the river to the New Jersey side, the south tower fell. He got off the ferry and found a park bench on the waterfront. At 10:28 am, he saw the north tower fall and the dust cloud envelop the city.

Then James walked into a local bar for the first drink in his whole life. "I didn't realize how profoundly that day had rattled the paradigms I existed under," he said. "I was a good church boy. I didn't drink and was raised to work hard, support my family. That day, I had six Long Island Iced Teas in three hours. I wanted an anesthetic, to forget."

In the immediate aftermath, James worked in the building across the street, every day seeing bodies being pulled from the rubble. "Again, I didn't realize how much that affected me. I was very good at blocking," he said. He thought he was managing well. He was doing some phone-based counseling through the Red Cross 800 number. A corporate weekend warrior, he traveled back to Ontario on the weekends to be with his family, but he was still in denial of his suffering. His family could see that he was not the same person. He was fearful of taking elevators in tall buildings, of planes flying low, and of airport security officers carrying guns. He began alternating between bouts of extreme isolation and striking out in anger. His family members were at their wits' end. They had no idea that this level of anger was a symptom of PTSD.

James's coping mechanisms finally wore down, and on a plane on September 11, 2005, he lost it. He thought he was having a heart attack. "It took me four years to the day before I had a full reaction." Afterward, he said, "I had more anxiety attacks. As my blood pressure was rising, I was dipping deeper into depression. I was suffering from hyperarousal all the time, and it was exhausting." James had to take a medical disability leave, and he lost his job when he returned. His marriage broke under the strain. He is now the custodial parent raising his children, ages thirteen, twelve, ten, and seven.

"PTSD is not a single event," he said. The divorce, the loss of his children and then the reestablishment of custody, and the loss of employment were accumulative. I knew his mother, and I could see the pain in her face when she talked about her son. He had been emotionally locked up for a long time.

How did James ultimately get help? James told his doctor he couldn't sleep. "I'm having nightmares. I'm having flashbacks to New York on 9/11," he said. The doctor gave him fourteen days of sleeping pills and said have a good night's sleep. The next step was antidepressants for twelve weeks. From his experience, James said, "Family physicians don't have a clue."

Asked if his pastor could be helpful, James says that he also didn't know how to deal with PTSD. Again, in James's experience, the pastor's response was, "Let's pray for you" or "Look to God for a miracle," but that didn't do anything for the anxiety attacks or the sense of impending doom. It actually left him feeling dismissed and abandoned.

James is now in the middle of counseling. He tells me that he has learned a lot since I made an appointment for him to get help. He didn't even think he had a problem until his company put him on that plane on September 11, 2005. He believes that strong denial is common to many men. He calls it "a guy thing, a cultural bias. Guys like to repress. Asking for help is considered a sign of weakness, and no man wants to admit weakness—come hell or high water." James's prime advice now to all the men out there who may be suffering from trauma is: "There is no shame in asking for help."

James is in a healing place. "In the midst of all this, I remembered an analogy I once heard," he said, with insight into his own blindness. "I don't know who discovered water, but it wasn't a fish." Nothing in our culture trains us to understand this.

Dave

Dave Buck is the CEO of Coachville, the world's largest hub for life, business, and executive coaches, with membership currently at more than 65,000, in more than 175 countries. I met Dave at a seminar he conducted in Toronto in 2005.

Dave's experience with trauma was a hard series of multiple emotional hits over a period of six months, beginning with the death of his dear friend Thomas Leonard. Leonard was the founder of Coach U and Coachville and is considered to be the "Father of Coaching" worldwide. Leonard died in 2003 at age forty-seven and left the company to Dave. Dave was thrown into the job with little preparation in corporate management—nor the legal challenges that followed almost immediately after.

Two former employees of the business sued Dave. Another person who had made a previous deal with his friend Thomas sued him. His friend's estate decided to sue him, which meant that the decision about the future of the company could stay in probate for four years. Dave had never been in a lawsuit in his life. Now he had three on his hands.

To compound the grief of losing his best friend and the problem of the lawsuits, Dave's girlfriend of ten years left him to marry someone else. This was just too much to bear, and he was just hanging on by a thread until he finally snapped. He said, "I couldn't take it any more. I was ready to just disappear."

Dave's friends noticed his unraveling. They urged him to seek professional help. "They told me," he recalled, "you are not going to get out of this depression, Dave, unless you see a doctor. The spiral you're in will just spin you out of control." All this was news to Dave, because, as he said, "I've always been a very upbeat person, and I never thought I'd ever be depressed. I just figured I was having a bad streak."

Dave's friends suggested that he should seriously look at taking anti-depressants, since they had both used them successfully. He told both of them that he was not comfortable taking those kinds of drugs. His approach to his health had always been more holistic. His friends knew this, but they assured him that it was not so bad and that it didn't have the stigma it used have.

I met Dave at the seminar he was leading in Toronto shortly after he "snapped." The seminar was restricted to twenty people, which I thought was unusual, since I had heard him speak in front of very large audiences a couple of times. He is a very dynamic speaker, which was why we were there. For some reason, I asked him to join us for lunch. I had just started the Post Traumatic Stress Disorder Association; in fact, my business cards were literally still wet. While I was telling my story about my struggle with PTSD, he recognized some of his own symptoms. Coincidence? I don't think so. It was fate. He needed help, and I had come into his life to direct him toward getting it. After a long discussion, I found him an EMDR specialist in his area, and when I received his e-mail months later thanking me for saving him, my feeling of gratitude for being able to help was overwhelming. He would have taken his friends' advice and not gone the EMDR treatment route. Dave started therapy in November. The next four months were intense but very productive.

Dave calls EMDR miraculous. "That's when I started getting better," he said. His therapist confirmed that he was depressed and that he had PTSD, and then they went to work. Dave described his state going into the sessions as being "stuck." He couldn't resolve logistical issues. "Anything more than two steps," he says, "I couldn't handle. As soon as I got to the third step, my brain got all scrambled. And here I was, trying to run a large organization."

Through EMDR treatments, Dave was able to identify issues, past and present, that were upsetting him. He was able to face his anger and anxieties. He recalls a defining moment in late October, when he came home and couldn't get his key in the door. Frustrated and powerless, he stood alone, crying in front of his house.

As he learned more about himself, he was able to release the events that had clogged his system and blurred his responses. He could actually feel the re-patterning taking place inside, his brain rewiring and the mind-body connection being restored. "By February, I was feeling pretty good," he said. "That was a rapid turnaround month. I started really exploring myself. And from there, I could take an accelerated path to recovery."

Dave credits EMDR and his therapist with providing a baseline of recovery from which he could put his life back in order. He says his optimistic view on life ironically turned into a curse, because it blinded him to his own distress. He had always believed in the super-individualist adage, "If it's to be, it's up to me." He thought he could do everything all by himself. He learned otherwise, and the lesson was freeing.

Stress melted away. His recovery took off, with coaching techniques kicking in after he had reached the baseline with EMDR. "I had a lot of cleanup to do," he said. He asked his two personal coaches to help him to right the personal and business mistakes he had made. He applied his coaching skills, especially environmental design, to make sure he stayed healthy and on track. "Being depressed for years, I had not taken care of the people who love me," he states. He started to mend fences, reestablishing relationships he had neglected. He sees himself as much more compassionate and capable because of this experience.

Dave is quick to point out that "you cannot coach someone out of PTSD." It's a powerful statement from a leader in the coaching business. But coaching is very useful after the hard inner work is done, what he refers to as the "time in the darkness" when he discovered that "sweet Dave Buck had an evil twin inside, and he was no fun."

He has come to believe that out of this dark comes the possibility of real enlightenment. "It's the yin and yang inside of yourself. You have to be able to embrace both to be truly whole and enlightened," he says. "And I can now see when someone else is in the darkness too, because I know what it looks like, and I have an appreciation for it." He jokes, "I don't recommend PTSD, but it has made me a better person, a better coach. It's an incredible blessing. I have already referred three other people to EMDR therapists."

Here is Dave's final word: "We can be over-diagnostic about pathology in our culture. At the same time, PTSD is a real thing. If you are in any kind of helping profession, you should know what it is."

Suzanne

Suzanne Harrill is a professional counselor and author. For more than twenty-five years, she has been familiar with the pain of others. In an article entitled "Murder Visits My Family" in the Fall 2006 edition of her newsletter, *Innerwords Messenger*, she wrote of her own distress and the grieving process that follows:

> When I learned that my dear brother Richard, age 56 and in good health, was shot and killed, I started hyperventilating and could not catch my breath. The message delivered by his twin, my sister, sent me into a panic attack. I had to get off the phone to steady myself and practice breathing techniques learned over the years, such as breathing slowly as if I were blowing up a balloon. I heard my own voice talking to me as I had done in times past for others, mainly clients wanting techniques to manage their stress level.
>
> Lucky for me, my dog was outside when my husband was on his way to go mountain biking where there would be no phone signal. He returned to the house to put Dot inside, to find me crying and not right. I was sitting in a chair in the kitchen and managed to say, "Richard is dead, shot and killed at work last night." He immediately covered me with his arms, as I was stooped over sobbing, confused, and in shock. Soon, I called my sister back to gain some sense of this message and confirm what my ears had heard from

her, wanting to believe this was not true. I really could not believe this was true. While talking to Nancy on the phone, my husband booked me on a flight to my home state to be with my mother and sister. Six hours later, I was sitting in my mother's living room as we comforted each other.

Being together with loved ones was instrumental in helping me live through the first few days of emotional pain, as my chest was hurting so much. My sister and I spent almost every minute together the first week, which helped both of us. Sleep was almost out of the question at first. I calmed my restless body and mind with a mantra, a spiritual statement repeated countless times. As I breathed in silently, I said to myself, "God is," and as I breathed out, I said, "I am."[28]

After the initial shock, Suzanne felt waves of powerful emotions: sadness because her brother's teenage daughter, who lived with her mother and stepfather, would not get to know her dad as she grew up; sadness and anger because she couldn't continue to talk to Richard every week; anger because the police had produced no clues and no leads as to why someone would shoot Richard in the head and chest as he worked late at night at his talent agency. When found, he was still holding a pen in his hand. She experienced more anger at the amount of work required when a sudden death occurs—not just the criminal investigation, but the probate requirements, sorting of documents, record keeping, and death certificates. "I had no idea," she says. She was angry that these worldly affairs kept her from grieving for her lost brother.

Suzanne still wakes up in the middle of the night, "going over and over things you can't do anything about." Circular thinking is part of the grieving process. She says that the admonition to "get over it" is impossible at first, because you are in it. Her advice is to experience it fully, knowing that you will come out on the other side eventually. And her pain was doubled, because at the same time as Richard's death, her mother was diagnosed with lung cancer. Her eighty-two-year-old mom is optimistic and undergoing treatment. She wants to live, because after Suzanne's father's death ten years ago, she found another partner to love. Suzanne wants her to continue to enjoy her life and jokes with her mom. "I've told her she can't go this year. It would be too rough on us."

"Us" includes Suzanne's younger sister, Nancy, also a therapist and Richard's twin. "I am so blessed in life," she says, "to have a sister with the same profession and who is on the spiritual journey with me." Suzanne's mother and sister live in Maryland, where Richard lived too. Suzanne lives with her husband in Colorado. Their three grown daughters were very supportive at the funeral and during the immediate aftermath. Although separated by distance, the family has always been very close emotionally. Suzanne calls this a great benefit to healing from a traumatic loss. She understands the other side too. "I've talked with people who lost family members, and they didn't have good memories. I think they have a deeper grief, because they never had what they wanted from that person. I think it is important to allow yourself to have those thoughts and not suppress them."

Suzanne writes eloquently about self-awareness and affirmation in her books and articles. She knows emotions and has a unique ability to teach herself and others how rich and compassionate life can be. "Self-care is important in my life, with or without tragedy," she says. "I'm kind of an obsessive-compulsive type, so I'm big on physical fitness and exercise every day, which calms 'flight or fight' urges in my body. Being in nature is helpful too."

In the grieving process, she recommends that you connect with loved ones and let friends be there for you. "Accept the kind ears of people. Don't stop talking about the person because he or she is no longer here. Listen, and remember as many positive stories as you can round up from other people. And finally, don't isolate yourself."

Share Your Life

James, Dave, Suzanne, and I came from very different traumatic experiences. However, we were each left with the same sense of loss of control and loss of self-worth, and we stopped functioning as we had before. We were lost and trapped in our own bodies, where the memories were stored. We each needed to put them to rest within ourselves and to put them to use in a healthy way. We wanted our futures.

CHAPTER FIVE

Unclutter Your Environment

Making room for the new

While I was getting my inner life in some semblance of a new order, I became keenly aware of all the chaos in my immediate physical environment—the layers of clutter I had accumulated physically, in my finances, and in my spirit. I tried to deal with it every single day. As a perfectionist at heart, this was a huge struggle for me. I couldn't concentrate long enough on one room or chore to finish a simple task.

This is typical PTSD behavior, and it holds the danger of reversing your own personal progress. I cannot stress this enough. You can't function at your full potential when you are inundated with your own clutter. You can't attract anything new if your spaces at home and the office are filled with irrelevant clutter. It crowds out the positive, and it must go. You must make room for the new.

Clearing the clutter in outward areas is really a form of emotional cleansing. It is as necessary and habitual as brushing your teeth every day, or taking out the dog, or washing your hair.

Did you know there are twenty-nine definitions of the word "clean"? Here are my top ten:

1. Free from dirt or impurities
2. Containing no foreign matter or pollutants
3. Not infected or diseased
4. Freshly laundered or washed after use
5. Just and fair
6. Morally pure and upright
7. Simple and flowing in design
8. Complete and unqualified
9. Cleared of weeds and unwanted undergrowth
10. Free from addiction

Everyone can probably agree that the above characteristics are desirable. You might even say they may be a bit too ideal. After all, life has its negatives too. Look at the opposites of "clean" in the list above: dirt, pollutants, infections, diseases, soiled laundry, injustice, unfairness, despicable morals, bad design, incomplete, incompetent, full of weeds and brush, trapped in addictions. Make your own additions to this list. Not a pretty picture, is it?

Clutter

Clutter is a funny thing. It has a life of its own, and it seriously zaps your energy. It is demanding and persistent. When you leave the house or office, it comes along. It could be the stuff you have not looked at in years: clothes that are not in mint condition, that no longer fit or don't look good on you, but they still crowd your closet; books in the basement that haven't been picked up and looked at in years, taking up precious space; equipment that has not worked for ages; poor lighting that has never been fixed. The list goes on and on.

There is grave risk in changing yourself inside and not changing your personal environment. You can fool yourself when you are away at a seminar or conference or vacation (in an uncluttered space) and you return home (to a cluttered space). You are ready to start anew, but nothing has changed at your old setting, and you can slip back into old patterns and dilute the progress you have made. Believe me, if nothing changes at home, you will continue to come back to your own messes, and they will affect you in a negative way. They can take you down. I know, because I struggled with keeping breathing space, which I continually stress in my Power of One discovery program. There is more information in the Resources section of this book.

Once you are aware of the fact that clutter in your physical environment creates a cluttered mind, it's time to get started. You can start small, even if it's just a drawer every day or a room every month, but it's important for you to start. Expect the cleanup to be hard, physically daunting at times—but know it is also a critical and courageous act of life change. It is as significant as making a move to a new house or cleaning out the home of a deceased relative. In effect, you are honoring the new you that needs more space to expand and grow.

Making Space

I'd like to share the steps I teach (and use myself) to help others to rid themselves of the unnecessary stuff in their physical environment.

Many people find this overwhelming, but if you do it one step at a time, it is less so. You may also find it beneficial to ask someone close to you to help you, and there are professional organizers for those who really feel that they absolutely can't do it without some outside assistance. This process will take time, so don't expect to finish it all in one day. It is, after all, part of your journey.

1. Go through your house or apartment twice, room by room (including your basement, garage, etc.)

The first time through, throw out all items that are of no value to anyone and are broken. The second time, pull the items that have some value, but no longer to you. Donate these to your favorite charity. You have to be honest with yourself. A lot of times, things are kept because you think you might need them in the future or that someone you know might need them. A good rule of thumb is that if you haven't used it in the last year, you need a good reason to keep it, because you're not likely to use it, and it's just taking up space. If you're not sure, put it in a box sealed with tape and mark it with a date six months from now. On that date, if you haven't opened the box, you will know that you need to donate the items. Repeat this process until there is nothing around that you feel you no longer need.

2. Go through the same process at your office.

Take a look at your files. Files have to be well organized for fast retrieval. In this fast-moving world, you can't afford to get frustrated and overwhelmed. Disorganized documentation impedes progress and demotivates.

3. Free yourself of the frustration of broken equipment at home and at the office.

Are your appliances, machinery, equipment, and car working well? Notice immediately when something is in less than good order. Repair or replace it right away, or have an expert do it for you.

4. Upgrade your computer, your tools, and your equipment on a regular basis.

Upgrading computers, tools, and other equipment can be costly. It would be wise to establish a budget for these upgrades, to allow you to take advantage of the latest technologies without breaking the bank.

5. Examine the lighting at your home and office.

Good lighting plays an important role in your well-being, especially in the winter months when there is less daylight; this is especially important for people who suffer from seasonal affective disorder (SAD). These people are affected by fall's and winter's short days and long nights, which may trigger feelings of depression, lethargy, fatigue, and other problems. The Mayo Clinic suggests, among other treatments, to "let there be light, by making your spaces sunnier and brighter, by opening blinds, adding skylights and trimming tree branches that block sunlight."[29]

6. Now take a look at your clothes.

Do they fit? Are they out of date? Are they in good repair? And most of all, do they make you feel terrific? This is one place a friend or someone close to you can really help. Ask her to be totally honest, and trust what she tells you. It's okay to get rid of the old clothes—you're making room for the new.

Take your time! Look at this process for what it is: a positive move to simplify your life.

Address whichever area is most important to you right now.

Success in one area will already help you feel more complete, and you'll be eager to address the other areas. Then you'll have the clarity to arrange the contents in your home and office the way it suits *you*. You will begin to have more and more energy, which will open the door to ridding your other environments of their less-than-perfect aspects.

Again, keep your environment clear of unnecessary stuff. It will simplify your day-to-day life. This is one of the cardinal rules of my new life. Inevitably, clutter will come again. Like a weed, it always grows back. You just have to make sure it goes away, too. There is no question that humans are the consummate consumers and that everyone loves stuff. Discrimination needs to precede any purchase. Periodic cleaning is not only a physical action; it is also the maintenance of sound mental health. I love to walk into my house when it is clean and airy. The feeling of plentiful interior space is inviting. I am as welcomed by my own home as I am by my wonderful pets. The great bonus is that there is also ample room to welcome friends to enjoy the space with me.

Using Your Space

Once there is space, another factor comes into play. What is in my space? How is it positioned? Do I like it? This is why the feng shui movement has taken off in the Western world. In the West, people understand the need for space, but they don't know how to preserve it. Generally, they try to fill it up with things—like filling silence with words, verbal clutter. But you can destroy the tranquility you seek. There is another way.

Everyone feels a sort of disconnect when they feel uncertain about where to put their furniture when they move into a new apartment or house. Will my things fit into the new space? Should I move the couch over here? Or there? How does it go with the rest of my furnishings? Or after living with the arrangements we have, we start to feel uncomfortable. Something is just not right. It feels jumbled or claustrophobic. Do you have too much stuff?

Literally translated, "feng shui" means wind and water, two elements that are always in flux. One of its theories is that energy is all around us and that building (or arranging) things in a space can affect how the energy flows. Following feng shui principles would mean an increase in positive energy, leading to an increase in well-being.

Again, sometimes a simple change can alter the whole disposition of a room and its occupants—like repositioning a mirror or changing a door opening. I use these basic concepts in my own home and office. In fact, I hired a feng shui practitioner to suggest the placement of furniture in my homes and office. I have found that my new arrangements make me feel calmer, and I thoroughly enjoy sharing these special spaces with others. They are not only clean and uncluttered; they are also harmonious, sacred. Our physical spaces reflect our spiritual selves. It isn't a one-way flow.

T. R. Raphael[30] says in *Feng Shui Step by Step,* "Your home breathes like a living body. Its breath ... comes in and out through the doors and windows and flows through corridors and rooms. When it flows unobstructed, it imparts the sensations of ease and comfort. But when its flow is obstructed due to clutter, the opposite happens: [it] becomes obstructed, the elements in your body become unbalanced, and your health and affairs suffer."

There are many excellent books about feng shui. To learn more about it, please check the Resources section of this book.

Take Charge of Your Finances[31]

An important part of the uncluttering process involves taking a deep look at your financial environment. Too many people are burdened by financial commitments and lifestyles they hang on to for the wrong reasons. If you lose sleep over financial worries, a time-out is required to get them in a state of repair, or at to least develop a plan to do so.

Worries about money take up an inordinate amount of time and emotional energy. You cannot have a clear mind and good health with extreme stress about monetary concerns. Once you have a plan, follow through. The purpose of having a plan is to learn to manage your money instead of letting money manage you.

The first step is to pay attention. How healthy is your financial environment? Don't know? Hmm ... maybe it's time for a close look.

There is power in knowing the details. This means knowing exactly how much money you earn and how much you spend. You might find out that your life is consumed by your lifestyle or that things are better than you thought.

The late Thomas Leonard, who is considered to be the father of coaching, posed a question in his book *The Portable Coach.*[32] "How much energy does your lifestyle consume? Is your lifestyle too big? What amount of time and money do you need to sustain it?"

If "living large" has become a driving force, it is standing between you and the life you want. Simplify. There is nothing wrong with having a lifestyle, as long as you make sure that it does not have you. Choosing lifestyle over life is about having more rather than becoming more—and being glorified for the role you're playing, not for who you are.

To get a life means that there is room to enjoy. You can have a really big life and a big lifestyle, but only if the lifestyle is not costing you excessively in time, emotion, space, risk, pressure, and adrenaline. And that's how more becomes less.

It's really amazing how more and more people I talk to are no longer willing to uphold a lifestyle that is driven mainly by material possessions, objects that are used to validate their success. They realize that most of their pleasures in life come from the simple things, such as watching a sunset and being with family and friends—real friends, the ones who hang out with you because of who you really are.

To create a financial environment that will support, not drain your energy, several things need to happen. Write down, to the penny, how much you earn, how much you spend every month, and what you are spending it on. Just knowing is very liberating. Then take an honest look at your scenario, since this will determine if you are living within your means.

Ask yourself, "Do I need to cut expenses?" Start with the big-ticket items. If you have debts, make a plan immediately to reduce them. Hire a financial coach to help you, if necessary. Use credit cards only as a substitute for carrying cash, not as a substitute for having the cash in the first place.

Most important of all, knowing your true financial status will allow you to take the appropriate actions to build up the financial side of your life, either by increasing your income or decreasing your expenses, or both. You can then start building a reserve. Once you have built up your reserve—always having six months' worth of living expenses in your bank account, enough to take a trip on the spur of the moment or pay for emergencies—you'll find a huge weight lift from your shoulders.

Stop Putting Up With Things

I had always operated under the notion that the more I was able to put up with, the stronger I would become. How wrong I was! There's nothing noble about putting up with things that annoy us. In fact, they drain our energy and depress us. Every time you put up with something, you feel less attractive to yourself.

As a baby, you did not tolerate anything; you were not going to put up with hunger, thirst, or dirty diapers. You made it known quite vocally that some action was required in order to satisfy your needs. But as you got older, you were told that looking after your own needs was selfish and that ignoring your own needs was "life."

The annoyances we tolerate are unlimited, and it is my intent to make you aware of the fact that they are not good for you. I encourage you to eliminate them one by one, keeping in mind that you might simply have to become accustomed to some. There may be some that you are unwilling to address, or you might feel that the cost of eliminating them is too high—like telling your mother-in-law that she cannot just appear on your doorstep whenever she feels like it.

If you are like most people, you are probably tolerating hundreds of things right now. It might be a "friend" who continually talks about his or her problems, or the people who come over for dinner and spend the entire evening talking about themselves. When they leave, they have absolutely no clue what you've been up to. You might have started to say something and were interrupted.

Other examples include the people who do not treat you the way you want to be treated at the office or at home, and the person who thinks his or her time is much more valuable than yours and is continually late. (I am getting a little hot under the collar as I write this.)

Maybe it is the spot on the rug or chipped paint that you walk by several times a day. It can also be the stuff you tolerate from yourself, like not honoring the commitments you have made to yourself or others.

When you start the clearing process, you will be amazed by the benefits you will experience. The first step is to buy a stack of three-by-five-inch cards. Write down the things you are tolerating in your life right now, one annoyance per card. Start with at least fifty items. The list should include the following areas: home, kids, spouse, "best" friend, job, your habits and behavior, others' habits and behavior, commute, television, e-mail, interruptions, and any other areas that apply to you personally.

Put the cards with the big nuisances into one pile and the smaller ones into another. Now start to eliminate them, one item at a time. Once you have eliminated an annoyance, rip up the card. You will find that the ripping action will not only give you a sense of accomplishment but also a great sense of relief.

In some cases, you will have to tell someone (in your usual smooth, effective, and nondisruptive way, of course) that you are no longer willing to put up with certain behavior, because it either hurts your feelings or annoys you right now. The card can be ripped up only when you see the positive change you expect.

You might want to start with a couple of the smaller items on your list, to help you build momentum, and then charge full steam ahead. In the best-case scenario, you will be able to accomplish this without causing a divorce or being fired from your job (unless that is what you have in mind).

Start today. Keep some cards near you at all times, so that you can add the things that annoy you as they occur to you. As you go through the process, you will find that you are developing higher standards for yourself and that you have more confidence. It might cause some upsets initially, including the fact that the things you used to fret about are no longer there—this can create a void for some people.

After three or four months, you will likely find that you have attracted some new people who are positive and stimulating and that the old complainers have distanced themselves, because they realize you are no longer putting up with things. Most of all, you will be calmer and more self-assured. You will also be proud of the fact that you have eliminated the annoyances that are within your control and communicated your needs to those around you.

Keeping a Journal

Everyone needs a "me file." One of the best ways to free yourself is to keep a journal. In her book *Journal to the Self,* Kathleen Adams, MA, calls the journal a seventy-nine-cent therapist. I can relate to that.[33] Writing down your feelings, negative and positive, will free your mind. This discipline might be hard at the beginning, but it is a way to create a dumping ground for your emotions. By putting your thoughts in writing, you move what's on your mind onto paper. It unclutters the mind. I use a journal to express my positive and negative emotions and feelings. I tend to use journals that are spiral-bound, because after I reread the negative stuff, I rip out the pages and tear them into shreds. I find that in itself to be extremely therapeutic and freeing. I have disciplined myself to write in my journal for at least fifteen minutes a day. I highly recommend this practice.

CHAPTER SIX

A New Destination

From a shattered belief system to a renewed spirit

We live in a "go" world. You try to keep on top of things, keep up with others—keep going at all costs. Everyone is fearful of stopping, even just for a while. Stopping might mean that you will be passed by and will no longer be in the game. Perhaps that is why everyone seems to hate stoplights, speed bumps, and anything that slows them down or gets in the way.

Trauma brings you to a dead stop.

And that is also a profound opportunity. Rebuilding your life after trauma reveals a whole new world. As I've said before, you can have a better life, but you may need help in order to build it. Once you start building it, you begin to see that your inner struggle is where the need for change is revealed, and perhaps then you are ready for the spiritual side of healing.

But to get there, you need to use the tools of trauma management. We've already discussed the first part of healing: dealing with the emotions and thought processes that arise from trauma. But no healing is complete without also addressing the spiritual and physical sides. I have found a lot of spiritual strength in Buddhism's principles, because they've answered my questions about suffering and imperfection. There is also a practical side to these teachings, and I found them in the form of breathing, meditation, and acupuncture.

In 1999, the same year as my accident, an article by Robert Grant, PhD,[34] was published in the e-journal *Traumatology*, entitled "Spirituality and Trauma." I only found his abstract this year when I was doing research for this book. He tells us that trauma can bring us to a new level of living in the spirit. In his conclusion, he writes, "Trauma, in spite of its brutality and destructiveness, has the power to open victims to issues of profound existential and spiritual significance. Trauma throws victims onto a path that mystics, shamans, mythic heroes and spiritual seekers have been walking for thousands of years. The difference is that victims of trauma must work this territory or be overcome by it."

Robert Grant says that at these times, "the ego is displaced or cracked open … Trauma demonstrates that the ego (the rational aspect of consciousness) cannot contain or make sense of certain aspects of life." I was there. And I was terrified.

Most of us, especially in the Western world, have been taught that the ego is the essence of being human. It is not. Grant states, "The ego is a precarious construct. Trauma either displaces or obliterates the ego. Victims are thrust into the realm of the Deeper Self without warning and preparation. This brutal exposure illuminates the fact that the ego is a mosaic held together by personal narration, continual feedback from others and internalised object relations. Exposure to its lack of unity and substance is terrifying. Some do not recover from this forced encounter with a space in consciousness referred to as the 'great Naught' or nothingness. Some decompose and others fragment. This is the realm from which both mystics and madmen emerge."

And, I would add, regular people like me. But something else has been added to me: a depth of compassion for others, which I had not reached before. Before, I had compartmentalized myself as a self-contained human being around which the universe rotates; I had a kind of "master of the universe" image of myself. Notwithstanding all the current images of superheroes, there is no such person in reality.

We can all be broken, overwhelmed, and rendered powerless by traumatic events. Our health can be restored only through the assistance and trust of others. Deepak Chopra[35] has said in his book *The Deeper Wound,* "Healing is not a matter of solitary work." In our culture, to refuse to acknowledge this comes at great cost. My friends James and Dave had a hard time seeking help. I too was resistant. I encourage anyone reading this to ask for assistance, because our fundamental dependency on each other is the common ground for all emotional restoration—and spiritual transformation. I can't overemphasize the importance of this statement. Stop. Think about this as an opportunity of a lifetime—which it is.

Learning from Buddhism

The spiritual dimension of healing came to me gradually, probably because I was opening up in layers. Just as the negative reactions to PTSD had taken over my life for a time, positive qualities immediately started building up when I sought help. These led me to look east. All religions have to deal with the existence of suffering and the question of transcendence. I had been raised in the Christian church, but I was now drawn to a more meditative expression of belief, a place where I could pause and reflect. I needed silence.

I started reading books on Buddhism, and the following excerpt from the book *Transform Your Life* by the venerable Geshe Kelsang Gyatso[36] really resonated with me:

> All living beings have the same basic wish to be happy and avoid suffering, but very few people understand the real causes of happiness and suffering. People generally believe that external conditions such as food, friends, cars, and money are the real causes of happiness, and as a result devote nearly all their time and energy to

acquiring these. Superficially it seems that these things can make you happy, but if you look more deeply you shall see that they also bring us a lot of suffering and problems.

Happiness and suffering are opposites, so if something is a real cause of happiness it cannot give rise to suffering. If food, money, and so forth really are causes of happiness, they can never be causes of suffering; yet you can know from your own experience that they often do cause suffering. For example, a main interest is food, but the food you eat is also the principal cause of most of our ill health and sickness. In the process of producing the things we feel will make us happy we have polluted our environment to such an extent that the very air we breathe and the water we drink now threaten our health and well-being. Everyone loves the freedom and independence a car can give us, but the cost in accidents and environmental destruction is enormous. People feel that money is essential to enjoy life, but the pursuit of money also causes immense problems and anxiety. Even your family and friends, with whom you enjoy so many happy moments, can also bring a lot of worry and heartache.

In recent years our understanding and control of the external world have increased considerably, and as a result there is remarkable material progress; but there has not been a corresponding increase in human happiness. There is no less suffering in the world today, and there are no fewer problems. Indeed, it could be said that there are now more problems and greater unhappiness than ever before. This shows that the solution to our problems, and to those of society as a whole, does not lie in knowledge or control of the eternal world.

I began to go to classes taught by Kelsang Rabgye,[37] a Buddhist monk who teaches at the Mahayana Buddhist Center in London, Ontario. I wanted to know more about suffering, and the first of the Four Noble Truths in Buddhism is that life is suffering. Framing a question such as "Why do bad things happen to good people and good things happen to bad people?" seems irrelevant when suffering is universally experienced all the time. I thought I had come to the right place. I was starting to stretch spiritually.

The second fact of life I learned from Rabgye's teachings is that all living things, including human beings, are imperfect, interconnected, and impermanent. In other words, you make mistakes, everyone does it to one another, and life is short and continually changing. These three qualities are in direct contrast to how most have been taught to live. They are hard to swallow, for everyone has been taught a rugged individualism. It's all about oneself and one's perfection—one's accumulation of wealth or status. Relationships take a back seat. I become priority number one and others are to sustain me or get out of my way. People act like they will live forever, and they have delusions of grandeur and intimations of immortality.

People who stop and take the time to accept responsibility for their actions are those who can change. The inner struggle is where the real action is. You can blame everyone in sight, external circumstances or accidents, even God. But inside is where you turn your life around. That requires conscious awareness, looking in the mirror, and developing a spiritual practice that requires the same commitment as any other kind of practice, like exercise or learning the piano. It takes time and effort until it becomes habitual. Just like recovery from addiction, you can't become well until you say you are not well. Awareness is the first step to mending a broken spirit.

The third fact I learned is that this life of suffering is caused by attachment to negative instincts, and by either ignorance or denial of this attachment.

The fourth fact is that everything is impermanent and that change is the only constant in life. We ourselves change from day to day and year to year. Our relationships change, our possessions change, and everything is in a state of constant flux.

When I spoke to him about this, Kelsang Rabgye said, "Sometimes, for deluded reasons, we cling to our distress. We know it well. It gives us a special identity we wouldn't otherwise have." In other words, you may choose to cling to any trauma or negativity. This is heavy stuff. However, this is not about blame, or blaming the victim. Blaming is a useless activity. What it is about, Kelsang Rabgye said, is ignorance. "We engage in actions, but we don't know or care what or whom they are going to affect now or in the future. Actions produce results. This sense of morality gives us control over what will happen to us." Simply put, if it's true that negative thoughts produce negative effects, then it is equally true that positive thoughts produce positive effects. It's all cause and effect. Take your pick. Accept the outcome. Don't blame someone else.

A Buddhist cultivates the cause of happiness, which is to lead a life of benefit to others. This is an empowering idea. It gives you the power to change and create your own future, because you are taking the concerns of others into consideration. Instead of a myopic view of "me," it opens up the whole vista of our relationship to all humanity. You see yourself as an actor on a universal scale—not because you are Superman or Wonder Woman, but because you belong to others, as they belong to you. The beauty of a Buddhist path is that it is the road to hope, to a compassionate heart and mind. As Kelsang Rabgye states, "It can change everything."

Breathing

Several people have asked me what the single most helpful thing I learned during my journey of recovery was, and I have to say that it was paying attention to my breathing. In Buddhism, the wholeness of a human being is celebrated—and used. You are called upon to be aware, to pay attention to your life and the lives of all those around you. And you are called upon to make intentional, positive moves. One way to facilitate this process—and you don't have to be a Buddhist or a yogi—is to literally learn to breathe again, this time using the many forms of breathing given the body at birth. On the simplest level of existence, you breathe autonomously already. Your body does it for you. Breath is what keeps you alive. Take it away, and you die. In a 24/7 technologically based world, have you noticed that when you are stressed out, you stop breathing, or your breath becomes very shallow, or you start to breathe faster and faster and wind up hyperventilating? This sends your stress level soaring, and you can bring on a full-blown anxiety attack.

The practice of breathing anew goes back thousands of years. It is a central factor in times of stress, as it is in quiet moments of meditation. The concentration on the breath, listening to it, breathing deeply, intentionally, continues to be a major tool to use to reach inner awareness during meditation and calming your body and mind today. Jon Kabat-Zinn says in his book *Full Catastrophe Living*[38] that "mindfulness of breathing is central to all aspects of meditation practice." He says that there are two ways of practice. One involves the formal discipline of making a specific time in which you stop all activity. This helps to naturally deepen your ability to keep your attention on the breath, which will improve your ability to concentrate in general as the mind becomes more focused and calmer for a longer period of time. The second way of practicing using the breath is to be mindful of it from time to time during the day. This way helps with meditative awareness and physical relaxation. I find both methods to be equally effective.

You are probably accustomed to Western medicine's reliance on other ways to reach these states, primarily through the administration of drugs to lower anxiety or alleviate depression. Very few doctors teach patients how to breathe more effectively, perhaps because they see this as a religious responsibility, not a medical concern—at least until CPR, a tracheotomy, or a ventilator is required to save a life. In Christian traditions, the role of the breath is acknowledged in biblical terms, such as God blowing his breath into the first humans. The intellectual underpinning, the theology, is there, but the practice has diminished. You are not taught how to breathe in church.

In Buddhism and other traditions, the practice is alive and well. Maybe that is why people in the West are attracted to it. Learning to breathe more fully, to be able to use your body more effectively day to day and in times of crisis, is an affirmation of the control you have been given as a human resource. For PTSD, breathing aids in regulating the heartbeat, clearing the mind, relaxing tension, and sustaining overall health. These simple steps all contribute to growth and to learning compassion for ourselves and for others.

I know it is a lot easier to write about this than to do it. I also know that it works, because I can see the difference between before and after. This is not an esoteric philosophy or mental gymnastics.

Another technique is meditation. To me, meditation is an "attention asset." It corrects the attention deficit experienced today, when everyone feels fractured in time, jumping from thought to thought, place to place, and project to project. Meditation says to be still and just listen. Sometimes, you have become so accustomed to your anxieties that being still may be the hardest lesson to learn. When you can stop and focus, you can then be intentional and proactive in leading your life. You are not buffeted by the storms of your emotions or the events in your life, because you can let go of them.

If your experience is anything like mine, after practicing meditation for some time, you'll become more resilient, because you will plan time to pause and take stock and decide to take a positive approach to life. If you have ever been in a room filled with people meditating in silence, or chanting the same sounds together, the restorative energy is palpable, visceral. You are one with everyone, and you are gifts to each other. Reading the teachings of the Buddha can introduce you to a new way of living your life, even folding it into your present religious affiliation. He looked upon everyone he met as fellow travelers in a life that can transcend suffering and be filled with compassion. He invited them to sit with him for a while. And he welcomed them on their way.

You don't have to be Buddhist to enjoy meditation. Try to begin simply; it will be difficult at first. Set aside some time when you will be without interruptions. Some people find that it is easier to begin in the morning, before the rush of the day. Then find a quiet, clutter-free place and begin by listening to your breathing. You may find it useful to just allow your thoughts to wander at first as you focus on one central idea. There are many books and CDs that can help you get started, but the most important thing is to get started.

Acupuncture: A Holistic Approach

In Chinese traditional medicine, there are 365 pressure points and twelve meridians within your body. An acupuncturist's first step is to scan the whole body with his hand to find the place of abnormal tension or blockage. He then applies a pattern of acupuncture treatment to reopen the flow.

George Tsukahara[39] is a local general practitioner of acupuncture, which is a component of traditional Chinese medicine. This method of healing has been in existence for thousands of years and is based on the belief that the mind and body are not separate. They are the complementary energies of the whole universe of the individual. As George told me, "When something is wrong in the body, it affects the mind, and vice versa." I have been going to George for several years to relieve ailments associated with PTSD and day-to-day living. After each treatment, with the tiny needles inserted in the skin at precise points on the meridians, I feel a calming and an elimination of pain. This may be hard to explain to Westerners, especially since many have an understandable fear of needles. Normal hypodermic syringes are scary, deeply invasive, and hurtful.

George described the difference between Western medicine and Eastern medicine and their mutual alliance. "Western medicine is based on what is visible—what you can see, such as X-rays, MRIs, microscopic images. These procedures are the basis of our many tests. Eastern medicine is based on something you can't see, the chi—the life energy flow." To make this clear, he said that if you are bleeding, you go to Western medicine. If you feel poorly and you go to the doctor and he can't find anything, Eastern medicine may help. He said, "I don't have to see the problem. As long as I can feel whatever the person is complaining about, I can restore a balance to the whole system and alleviate the discomfort."

Acupuncture is becoming more integrated into Western medical practice. There are more and more scientific studies being undertaken on its value. However, one of the stumbling blocks for the strict scientist is that the foundation for acupuncture is a metaphysical, spiritual understanding of healing.

I was drawn to this form of healing because it opens up a vast landscape of human potential. It is not confined to one body part. It is accepting of pain that is not diagnosable by traditional tools or theories, and it values human intuition and human touch. There is an incredible lightness to it. You too may discover this if you find an acupuncturist in your area. Look in the yellow pages, or ask for recommendations. I've also put information in the Resources section at the end of this book. When you talk to them, you will get a sense of what they believe and whether that belief is compatible with yours.

I am amazed how the Buddhist way and acupuncture overlap many of the therapeutic experiences I have had. They have many things in common. Above all, I think they treasure time, not as a commodity or a dial on a clock, but as pure possibility for relationships to mend and blossom. They reach for a more spiritual dimension of time. Where meaning is paramount, your existence is validated and enhanced, and kindness becomes as reflexive as ancient responses to fear. You can give and receive affection and love at any time, because these gifts of the spirit are not limited in time and space. You cannot erase memories that paralyze, but you can honor them by living with compassion.

I thank my healers, my therapists, and my teachers for their support, guidance, and accompaniment on this journey of mind, body—and spirit.

CHAPTER SEVEN

The Fork in the Road

Trauma brings you to a fork in the road. The choice is yours

When you have suffered a trauma strong enough to lead to PTSD, you are at a fork in the road of life. You just may not realize it at the time. But as I've discussed in earlier chapters, you do have a choice—an important choice—between the positive and the negative.

This polarity is important, because the law of attraction dictates that you attract what you project, and this is the basis of one of the courses I teach, called the Attraction Program. The program is designed on the premise that we are all walking magnets and therefore attract what we project. Did you ever notice that when one thing goes wrong, it is often the start of a chain of unfortunate events? Conversely, everything in life often seems to be going right. This phenomenon is caused by the energy you project outward. When everything is right, you feel positive, and you attract more positive energy. The same happens when one thing goes wrong and you allow your negative reaction to attract more of the same.

The initial state of PTSD is strong emotional disarray—remember, the *D* in PTSD stands for "disorder." This is a negative state, and unfortunately, it makes you extremely vulnerable to its compounding effects. I know; it happened to me. You don't want to attract more negativity, so you need to start being proactive in protecting yourself.

It's called looking out for number one, and in this case, it's not a negative attribute. The laws of attraction apply, and others, many with good intentions, will seek you out with their own stories of trauma and loss. This is natural.

But my advice is to intentionally set very strong boundaries and interrupt this communication—the earlier on, the better. Otherwise you will be exhausted. You are already in overload, and your system can't sustain any more negative impact. Your comfort zone has shrunk dramatically, and that's perfectly normal. The thing is, most people aren't raised to think this way and don't feel that they should set limits like this, because it's being rude. But you should not feel guilty about it, because it's necessary and for your good. When I found myself in this situation, I just told myself, *I'm not Superwoman. I'm Ute, and Ute has limits right now.*

It takes hard work and constant effort to produce positive feelings. But this is the goal and the gold. This is when healing really begins. You become stronger and stronger as you move negativity aside and let the positive energy flow through. You can then start to rely on your strengths as you recognize your weaknesses. Only then are you able to share truly helpful directions with others.

Once you have passed this point, you can become a healer. People are drawn to you and you to them, but the reason is different. With the positive energy attracting you, you can now be compassionate toward others and share directions and point the way without losing some of your own self. Actually, you have an abundance of affirmation to share. When the negative turns to the positive, a shift occurs, and you, the student, become a teacher. You have the ability to become someone else's mentor, just as you were mentored. You are now seen as someone with knowledge and wisdom, someone who just might understand their situation and assist them.

You can help others relate and see the upside of the future, because when you have not only survived the ordeal but also are thriving, it can give them hope. Compassion and empathy contain large doses of positive energy and self-respect. These qualities are infectious and as potent as negativity is lethal.

This is really the final illustration of the impact that positive psychology can have on your life, even after you discontinue therapy. Dan Baker, the founder and former director of the Life Enhancement Program at Canyon Ranch Health Resort in Arizona, says, "The bottom line is that positive psychology is about what's right with human beings and their organizations and institutions. More specifically, it's the serious study of strength, character, and virtue. Subtopics under that are human resilience, optimism, and lifelong learning." Just listening to this description makes me feel more empowered. He goes on to say, "Happy people are proactive. So someone who has suffered trauma has to understand that it is very important to be proactive as soon as possible." ASAP. It's best to get help sooner, rather than later. Lingering passivity is a killer. "Go study the resilient people in the world, and you begin to see patterns emerge," he says. "First and foremost, resilient people consciously make a choice to become proactive. They look for lessons in the heartache.

"People who are resilient with PTSD have a sense of direction and a set of values of what is important in life. These values provide a foundation for engaging in everyday life. Resilient people are altruistic, not self-absorbed." This is what makes them so magnetic. They give of themselves because they have learned much and have much to give, more than they themselves need.

We are a long way from the "Why me?" question that can haunt survivors of a tragedy

In your heart of hearts, you know what's right in your life—as surely as those passengers going down in a Pennsylvania field knew that they wanted to say good-bye to those they loved. What it boils down to is trusting what is right in your life and building on it. Dan Baker says that one of the overall themes of Buddhism, which is strange and hard for people to grasp, is that "the world is perfectly the way it should be, given all the things that have come before it, and you are called to acceptance—not acquiescence—and awareness of this reality. Awareness comes first. You've got to have a clue."

It takes some time to come out of the negative state where you are asking yourself, "Why me?" But soon, a crossroads will emerge, and a choice will have to be made. Here lies the personal tipping point. One route is a loop road that repeatedly brings you back to the past. The other path is a winding, unknown way into the future. The happy person, the healthy, magnetic person, is the one who chooses the second path.

Healthy human beings, since the beginning of time, have been, by their nature, proactive builders. You construct relationships, family, career, and community. Why? Because you want to be connected to each other, to be productive on this earth. You want warmth along with strength, clarity with character, and laughter with virtue. You want to be able to bounce back from adversity and be a lifelong learner. Dan Baker says, "At the moment of conception, death is assured." That is a given, as is life, which has limited visiting rights on the planet. Time is precious, so you had better make the most of it.

It's easy to recognize a constructive, positive person when you meet her or him. They radiate what's right about our species. I would bet that all of these successful people have been immeasurably scarred by events in their lives. But those scars are their badges of beauty and tolerance and care. They wear them proudly, and they activate a huge magnetic field.

I strive to be one of them, and I hope that those who read this book find the courage to take the second path when they reach the forks in their lives.

CHAPTER EIGHT

The Power of You

Sustaining life beyond trauma

I have subtitled this chapter "Sustaining life beyond trauma" because it speaks to stations farther down the road from the initial trauma. Much of what I shared in the previous chapters was about ongoing processes. You may find that you need a lot of help when you start therapy, or you may only need a little bit. Clearing clutter and keeping the external aspects of life in order requires ongoing effort, or it will revert right back to where it was before. You always have to monitor your internal energy to keep a positive flow.

Seven years after my accident, I am back to building again. I'm building new organizations that have different goals, with different measurements of success. I'm building a book to serve as a guide to recovery. I'm trying to rebuild my relationships with family and friends on a more aware, caring foundation. I'm paying more attention to the effect of my actions on others. In a nutshell, I'm fully enrolled in the school of lifelong learning.

The term "sustainable" is used when talking about business, industry, or the natural world. It means keeping the organization or organism alive and well, so that it can continue to prosper—a kind of midwifery to creation. "Sustainable" is also a fitting term for defining daily life beyond trauma. You are not just maintaining something; you are sustaining, building, and feeding yourself.

The word *sustain* has numerous definitions, and they all apply. To sustain means all of these things:[40]

- •"To provide someone with nourishment or the necessities of life." Translation: eat right, care for your body.

- •"To keep something going with emotional or moral support." Translation: be proactive; honor your own best actions and those of others.

- •"To manage to withstand something and continue in spite of it." Translation: be courageous, and stand your ground in the face of opposition or adversity.

- •"To confirm that something is true or valid." Translation: be affirmative when you know it is right.

- •"To make something continue to exist." Translation: do your part to keep creation going.

Can you really develop your own sustainable life after trauma? I think so. You can cull the information you need to chart a fresh path. You can introduce new regimens to replace old habits. For example, you can certainly eat better. There is no problem with availability. The shelves of food markets are overflowing with fresh foods. You can build exercise into your daily routines. No more excuses that you don't have time. Time is all you do have, and you can't be in two places at the same time. You choose your priorities. If you want to take a good look at your life, write down how much time you spend doing what. This simple exercise may surprise you. It shows you what you value the most, where you choose to spend your precious time.

Another aspect of sustainability is keeping, not losing, your mind. Staying mentally and emotionally healthy does not mean that there will be no other traumas in your life. There will be. Count on it. Be prepared. You have resources within you that you have nurtured through your own experience, and you have found professional sources outside of yourself. These are the people to whom you refer others and whom you trust implicitly. Keep a list. Add to it. Use it when needed for your own peace of mind.

It also means that you have to accept that you live in a world of information overload.

Information is everywhere, from a plethora of niche magazines to googling anything and everything on the Internet, from hundreds of TV channels to bloggers galore to hundreds, perhaps thousands of podcasts in the offing, and much more to come from the communication geniuses and ad houses of tomorrow.

An open society and free media are good things. They relay the data and provide analyses, critiques, satires, research, and points of view, many shot through with commercial pitches and super graphics. They try to reach audiences, sell myriad products in print and online, pitch arguments, and influence others.

For those who have experienced trauma and are already overwhelmed by its effects, an overload of information may seem more of a burden than a help. You must proceed with caution and patience. Processing takes time.

One of the fallacies of the Information Overload Age is that if you have all of the information, you can choose the best way to proceed with your decision. This does not necessarily compute. Sometimes you know that your behaviors are counterproductive, but you don't change them. Education does not always lead to transformation. But knowing is a first step when you do change your mind; therefore, it is important.

To sustain yourself into the future, which is always uncertain and around the corner, I recommend seeking to learn more about what you love and being open about what you don't know. Be on the cutting edge of curiosity. That's how I came to study Buddhism and to be open to the Eastern medical practice of acupuncture. Try new things that interest or inform you. This kind of information sparks a chain reaction. One thing leads to another, because knowledge doesn't have a beginning and an end. The play is never over. There are many more insights to come.

I can't stress enough that the tremendous double power of trauma is underestimated. You underestimate the power of trauma to hurt, because your understanding of life to that point has been shallow and narrow; thus you are undone when disaster strikes. You also underestimate the power of trauma to enhance your life, because your belief system has soured. You have turned your back on your own goodness.

Disclaimers don't work here—if only I had been born rich, or to other parents, or had married the right person, or had not been in that accident, or … you fill in the blank. You can't wait for further studies of the problem. And guess what? You have the opportunity of a lifetime to make a rewarding life. PTSD has brought me here, and I believe it can bring others to a new, fresh lease on life.

Personal sustainability sounds fine in theory, but life is not academic. It is real flesh and blood. Have you noticed how you can experience an amazing breakthrough in a therapy session, and then later on, the effect wears off, and you feel that you need another booster shot of self-esteem or clarity or courage? People want quick fixes. But that is not the way of the world. The sands are shifting with each step you take. You must learn to be flexible as you walk this Earth. Some days, you struggle through fire or fog. Other times, you almost glide gracefully through the hours. Once you accept this new normalcy, this greater reality of a fluid existence, it is easier to spring back and move on. You breathe more easily.

Beyond trauma is wisdom beyond information. You don't need to be overcome by the proliferation of data; you can sort and select what you need. Like a good quilt, the patches of wisdom and compassion you sew together can keep you warm in the cold seasons and provide a place to rest in the sun. But you are the quilter; your hands must piece the fabrics and stitch them into your life. This is not a ready-made, predictable comforter. It's not made of whole cloth, and you can't buy it or borrow it from someone else. You have to fashion your life yourself. That is why it is such a unique and beautiful legacy.

At the beginning of this book, I spoke of my recovery from trauma in terms of a tree damaged by forces beyond its control. As an endnote, I would like to return to the image of the restored tree.

Each of us is like a tree of life, a vibrant, breathing symbol of creation. You are also part of a larger forest of human beings, stretching toward the sun, receptive to the rains, vulnerable from start to finish.

I think that one of the most important things you learn as you grow your branches and repair your broken limbs is that you were invested with a remarkable power when you first came into this world. It is an inner power to re-root ourselves, to grow up with dignity, and to honor all those who share our humanity.

Emerson put it so well when he said, "The creation of a thousand forests is in one acorn."

Like every little acorn that falls from a tree, you and I are blessed each season with the potential to blossom and to harvest as well. Or, as Susanne Harrill has expressed in her poem, "Deep inside you know how to be you, as an acorn knows how to be a mighty oak."

The power of trauma finally translates into the power of you.

Then it will multiply into a thousand glorious forests.

Meet Ute Lawrence

Ms. Lawrence is an inspiring presenter and sought-after speaker. She is the founder of the Performance Enhancement Centre and the visionary behind the Power of One Discovery series, a profoundly transformational program designed to build a new foundation for personal and professional growth.

Ute herself experienced a life-changing moment. On a business trip to Detroit, she and her husband were in the center of the most horrific road accident in Canadian history. The near-death experience stopped her in her tracks. Very shortly after, she left her successful twenty-two-year career in the magazine publishing business to start a journey of self-discovery. This led her to establish the first civilian Post Traumatic Stress Disorder Association in North America and inspired her to write the book *The Power of Trauma.*

Ms. Lawrence is a Corporate Coach U graduate and a licensed practitioner of a number of powerful transformational programs, including the Attraction Program. She is a HeartMath one-on-one provider. HeartMath is a system of powerful, easy-to-learn, easy-to-use tools and technology to prevent, manage, and reverse the effects of stress.

In 2006, she founded the first civilian Post Traumatic Stress Disorder Association in North America. The association provides access to information about PTSD and a specific referral system lacking in many areas of medicine.

She is a member of the International Coach Federation, a founding member of the International Association of Coaches, a member of the Canadian Association of Professional Speakers, and a member of Rotary International.

Ute is a keynote speaker on the power of trauma. For more information, please visit www.ptsdassociation.com or www.powerofonediscovery.com.

Additional Web Resources

About PTSD

Healthy Place.com
http://www.healthyplace.com/communities/abuse/site/
post-traumatic_stress_disorder.htm
National Center for Posttraumatic Stress Disorder
http://www.ncptsd.va.gov/ncmain/ncdocs/fact_shts/
fs_what_is_ptsd.html
Canadian Mental Health
http://www.cmha.ca/bins/content_page.asp?cid=3-94-97
National Institute of Mental Health
http://www.nimh.nih.gov/
AD/HD Foundation of Canada
http://www.adhdfoundation.ca/

Acupuncture

The Chinese Medicine and Acupuncture Association of Canada
http://www.cmaac.ca/

EMDR

Eye Movement Desensitization and Reprocessing (EMDR) International Association
http://www.emdria.org/
EMDR Canada
http://www.emdrcanada.org/

EMDR Humanitarian Assistance Programs
http://www.emdrhap.org/home/index.php
EMDR Institute Inc.
http://www.emdr.com/

Cognitive Behavioral Therapy

National Alliance on Mental Illness
http://www.nami.org
The Centre for Cognitive Behaviour Therapy
http://www.ccbt.ca/

HeartMath

Institute of HeartMath
http://www.heartmath.org/
HeartQuotes from HeartMath
http://www.heartquotes.net/

Positive Psychology

Positive Psychology Centre
http://www.ppc.sas.upenn.edu/
Authentic Happiness
http://www.authentichappiness.sas.upenn.edu/Default.aspx

Feng Shui

The Feng Shui Association of Canada
http://www.fengshuiassociationofcanada.ca/main.html
Feng Shui Times
http://www.fengshuitimes.com/

Journaling

Self-help Healing Arts Journal
http://www.self-help-healing-arts-journal.com/index.html
Therapeutic Journaling

http://www.alternativedepressiontherapy.
com/therapeutic-journaling.html
Journalmuse.com
http://www.journalmuse.com/

Organizers

National Association of Professional Organizers (NAPO)
http://www.napo.net/
Professional Organizers in Canada
http://www.organizersincanada.com/

Suggested Reading

Adams, Kathleen. *Journal to the Self: Twenty-two Paths to Personal Growth.* New York: Warner, 1990.

Baker, Dan and Cameron Stauth. *What Happy People Know.* New York: Rodale, 2003.

Baker, Dan and Cathy Greenberg. *What Happy Women Know.* New York: Rodale, 2007.

Childre, Doc and Bruce Cryer. *From Chaos to Coherence.* Boulder Creek, California: Planetary Publications, 2000.

Childre, Doc and Howard Martin. *The HeartMath Solution.* New York: HarperSanFrancisco, 1999.

Chopra, Deepak. *The Deeper Wound: Recovering the Soul from Fear and Suffering.* New York: Harmony Books, 2001.

Grabhorn, Lynn. *Excuse Me, Your Life Is Waiting.* Charlottesville, Virginia: Hampton Roads, 2000.

Gyatso, Geshe Kelsang. *Transform Your Life: A Blissful Journey.* Conishead Priory
Ulverston, Cumbria, England:Tharpa Publications, 2001.

Kabat-Zinn, Jon. *Full Catastrophe Living: Using the Wisdom of Your Body and Mind to Face Stress, Pain, and Illness.* New York: Delta, 1990.

Kabat-Zinn, Jon. *Wherever You Go, There You Are.* New York: Hyperion, 1994.

Kasl, Charlotte. *If the Buddha Got Stuck.* New York: Penguin, 2005.

Leonard, Thomas J. *The Portable Coach: 28 Surefire Strategies for Business and Personal Success.* New York: Scribner, 1998.

Levine, Peter. *Waking the Tiger: Healing Trauma.* Berkeley, California: North Atlantic, 1997.

Matsakis, Aphrodite. *I Can't Get Over It: A Handbook for Trauma Survivors.* Oakland: New Harbinger, 1996.

Pearsall, Paul. *The Beethoven Factor: The New Positive Psychology of Hardiness, Happiness, Healing and Hope.* Charlottesville, Virginia: Hampton Roads, 2003.

Raphael, T. R. *Feng Shui Step by Step: Arranging Your Home for Health and Happiness.* New York: Three Rivers Press, 1996.

Weil, Andrew. *Healthy Aging: A Lifelong Guide to Your Well-Being.* New York: First Anchor, 2007.

Endnotes

[1] Matsakis, Aphrodite, *I Can't Get Over It: A Handbook for Trauma Survivors* (Oakland: New Harbinger, 1996).

[2] *National Post,* September 4,1999.

[3] *Ottawa Citizen,* April 2006.

[4] "Emotional and Psychological Trauma: Causes, Symptoms, Effects, and Treatment," *HelpGuide.org,* http://www.helpguide.org/mental/emotional_psychological_trauma.htm.

[5] National Center for Posttraumatic Stress Disorder, "What is Posttraumatic Stress Disorder (PTSD)?" *National Center for PTSD,* http://ncptsd.va.gov/ncmain/ncdocs/fact_shts/fs_what_is_ptsd.html.

[6] Levine, Peter, *Waking the Tiger: Healing Trauma* (Berkeley, CA: North Atlantic, 1997).

[7] Kabat-Zinn, Jon, *Full Catastrophe Living: Using the Wisdom of Your Body and Mind to Face Stress, Pain, and Illness* (New York: Delta, 1990).

[8] National Institute of Mental Health.

[9] National Institute of Mental Health, http://www.nimh.nih.gov/.

[10] EMDR International Association, http://www.emdria.org.

[11] Kasl, Charlotte, *If the Buddha Got Stuck* (New York: Penguin, 2005).

[12] All quotes in this chapter and throughout the book are from a phone interview on May 18, 2006, with Dr. Ruth Lanius, psychiatrist at Lon-

don Health Sciences Centre, London, Ontario, and Professor of Traumatic Stress, University of Western Ontario, London, Ontario.

[13] Weil, Andrew, *Healthy Aging: A Lifelong Guide to Your Well-Being* (New York: First Anchor, 2007).

[14] Weil, Andrew, *Healthy Aging: A Lifelong Guide to Your Well-Being* (New York: First Anchor, 2007).

[15] All quotes in this chapter and throughout the book are from a phone interview on May 17, 2006, with Dr. William Newby, clinical psychologist specializing in Cognitive Behavioral Therapy, in private practice in London, Ontario.

[1716] All quotes in this chapter are from interviews with Dr. Rollin McCarty (April 25, 2006) and Dr. Deborah Rozman (May 11, 2006) from the HeartMath Institute.

[18] Childre, Doc and Howard Martin, *The HeartMath Solution* (New York: HarperSanFrancisco, 1999), 10.

[19] Childre, Doc, *Freeze-Frame: A Scientifically Proven Technique for Clear Decision Making and Improved Health* (Boulder Creek, CA: Planetary Publications, 1998).

[20] Childre, Doc and Howard Martin, *The HeartMath Solution* (New York: HarperSanFrancisco, 1999), 74.

[21] All quotes in this chapter and throughout the book are from a phone interview on June 6, 2006, with Dr. Dan Baker, clinical psychologist specializing in Positive Psychology, founder and former director of the Life Enhancement Program at the Canyon Ranch, Arizona, and author of *What Happy People Know*, *What Happy Companies Know*, and *What Happy Women Know*.

[22] University of Pennsylvania, *Authentic Happiness: Using the New Positive Psychology*, http://www.authentichappiness.sas.upenn.edu/Default.aspx.

[23] Childre, Doc and Howard Martin, *The HeartMath Solution* (New York: HarperSanFrancisco, 1999), 266.

[24] Pearsall, Paul, *The Beethoven Factor: The New Positive Psychology of Hardiness, Happiness, Healing and Hope* (Charlottesville, VA: Hampton Roads, 2003).

[25] All quotes in this chapter and throughout the book are from a phone interview on May 2, 2006, with James Vail, systems analyst.

[26] All quotes in this chapter and throughout the book are from a phone interview on April 6, 2006, with Dave Buck, CEO of Coachville.

[27] All quotes in this chapter and throughout the book are from a phone interview on October 2, 2006, with Suzanne Harrill, MEd, licensed counselor and author of books on self-esteem, including *Seed Thoughts for Loving Yourself: Cultivating the Garden of Your Mind Day by Day.*

[28] *Innerworks Publishing.com*, "Transforming Victimization Story #9"

[29] "Seasonal Affective Disorder," *MayoClinic.com,* http://www. mayoclinic.com/health/seasonal-affective-disorder/DS00195/DSECTION=1.

[30] Simmons, T. R., *Feng Shui Step by Step: Arranging Your Home for Health and Happiness,* (Three Rivers Press, New York, 1996), 95.

[31] Lawrence, Ute. "The Power of Your Personal Environments," *LifeStyle* (March), 39.

[32] Leonard, Thomas J., *The Portable Coach: 28 Surefire Strategies for Business and Personal Success* (New York: Scribner, 1998).

[33] Adams, Kathleen, *Journal to the Self: Twenty-two Paths to Personal Growth* (New York: Warner, 1990).

[34] Grant, Robert, Ph.D., "Spirituality and Trauma," *TRAUMATOLOGYe* 5, no. 1, E2, (1999): 8–10.

[35] Chopra, Deepak, *The Deeper Wound: Recovering the Soul from Fear and Suffering* (New York: Harmony Books, 2001).

[36] Gyatso, Geshe Kelsang, *Transform your Life: A Blissful Journey* (Tharpa Publications, 2001), 5.

[37] All quotes in this chapter and throughout the book are from a phone interview on May 4, 2006, with Gen Rabgye Kelsang, London Mahayana Buddhist Centre, London, Ontario.

[38] Kabat-Zinn, Jon, *Full Catastrophe Living: Using the Wisdom of Your Body and Mind to Face Stress, Pain, and Illness* (New York: Delta, 1990).

[39] All quotes in this chapter and throughout the book are from a phone interview on June 6, 2006, with George Tsukahara, private practice of acupuncture, London, Ontario.

[40] *MSN Encarta World English Dictionary Online,* s.v. "sustain," http://encarta.msn.com/dictionary_/sustain.html.

978-0-595-46378-7
0-595-46378-9

Printed in the United States
122753LV00004B/53/P

9 780595 463787